THE ONE THING

WORKBOOK

This workbook is based on **The One Thing** book by Gary W. Keller and Jay Papasan. It will help you implement its message – focus on one thing and achieve all your goals. First, read the book (if you haven't already) to fully understand what, how, and why. Then use it as your daily journal/planner. It will last you for three months.

There are five different chapters:

1. *Daily success list* where you brain-dump all the things you think you should do, then narrow it to the most important 20 %, and finally, the one vital thing you should do that day. There are 92 success lists on 46 pages for daily use.

2. *Goal setting to the now* where you set your someday, five-year, one-year, monthly, weekly, and daily goals. That will help you define all your goals: from big-picture (purpose) to small-focus (priority). There are 46 pages – use them every other day.

3. *Improvement sheet* where you look for the one thing that needs to be done in all areas of your life (physical health, mental health, personal life, key relationships, career, and finances). There are 46 pages – use them every other day.

4. *Q&A sheet* will help you ask the right (great) question and also guide you to find the right (great) answer. There are 46 pages of Q & A sheets for you to use it as needed.

5. *Success habits sheet* where you check off each day (66 days) that you accomplish your new behavior/routine until it becomes a habit – a success habit. There are 3 sheets for you to establish 12 new success habits.

THE MAJORITY OF WHAT YOU WANT WILL COME FROM THE MINORITY OF WHAT YOU DO.

DAILY SUCCESS LIST

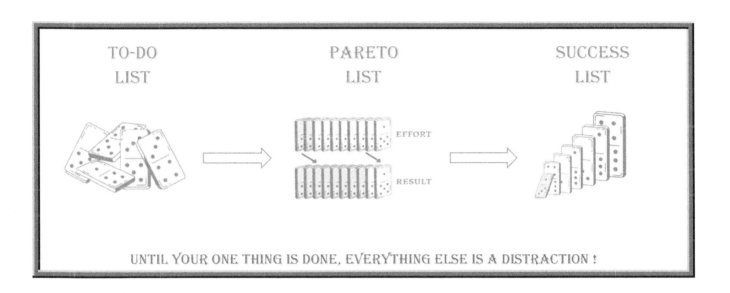

TO-DO
LIST

PARETO
LIST

SUCCESS
LIST

EFFORT

RESULT

UNTIL YOUR ONE THING IS DONE, EVERYTHING ELSE IS A DISTRACTION !

DAILY SUCCESS LIST

UNTIL YOUR ONE THING IS DONE,
EVERYTHING ELSE IS A DISTRACTION!

TO-DO LIST	PARETO LIST	SUCCESS LIST
A long list of the things you think you need to do.	The most important 20 % from the to-do list.	The ONE THING you have to do.

THE MAJORITY OF WHAT YOU WANT
WILL COME FROM THE MINORITY OF WHAT
YOU DO.

DATE:

TIME BLOCK:

From: _____ To: _____

Notes:

_____
_____
_____
_____
_____
_____
_____

TO-DO LIST	PARETO LIST	SUCCESS LIST
A long list of the things you think you need to do.	The most important 20 % from the to-do list.	The ONE THING you have to do.

THE MAJORITY OF WHAT YOU WANT
WILL COME FROM THE MINORITY OF WHAT
YOU DO.

DATE:

TIME BLOCK:

From: _____ To: _____

Notes:

_____
_____
_____
_____
_____
_____
_____

EFFORT

RESULT

DAYDREAMERS PRINT

DAILY SUCCESS LIST

UNTIL YOUR ONE THING IS DONE,
EVERYTHING ELSE IS A DISTRACTION!

TO-DO LIST	PARETO LIST	SUCCESS LIST
A long list of the things you think you need to do.	The most important 20 % from the to-do list.	The ONE THING you have to do.

TO-DO LIST

PARETO LIST

SUCCESS LIST

THE MAJORITY OF WHAT YOU WANT WILL COME FROM THE MINORITY OF WHAT YOU DO.

DATE:

TIME BLOCK:

From: _____ To: _____

Notes:

TO-DO LIST	PARETO LIST	SUCCESS LIST
A long list of the things you think you need to do.	The most important 20 % from the to-do list.	The ONE THING you have to do.

THE MAJORITY OF WHAT YOU WANT WILL COME FROM THE MINORITY OF WHAT YOU DO.

DATE:

TIME BLOCK:

From: _____ To: _____

Notes:

DAYDREAMERS PRINT

DAILY SUCCESS LIST

UNTIL YOUR ONE THING IS DONE,
EVERYTHING ELSE IS A DISTRACTION!

TO-DO LIST	PARETO LIST	SUCCESS LIST
A long list of the things you think you need to do.	The most important 20 % from the to-do list.	The ONE THING you have to do.

TIME BLOCK:

From: _____ To: _____

Notes:

_____

_____

_____

_____

_____

_____

_____

THE MAJORITY OF WHAT YOU WANT
WILL COME FROM THE MINORITY OF WHAT
YOU DO.

DATE:

TO-DO LIST	PARETO LIST	SUCCESS LIST
A long list of the things you think you need to do.	The most important 20 % from the to-do list.	The ONE THING you have to do.

TIME BLOCK:

From: _____ To: _____

Notes:

_____

_____

_____

_____

_____

_____

_____

THE MAJORITY OF WHAT YOU WANT
WILL COME FROM THE MINORITY OF WHAT
YOU DO.

DATE:

  EFFORT RESULT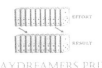

DAILY SUCCESS LIST

UNTIL YOUR ONE THING IS DONE,
EVERYTHING ELSE IS A DISTRACTION!

TO-DO LIST	PARETO LIST	SUCCESS LIST
A long list of the things you think you need to do.	The most important 20 % from the to-do list.	The ONE THING you have to do.

TIME BLOCK:

From: _____ To: _____

Notes:

_____
_____
_____
_____
_____
_____

THE MAJORITY OF WHAT YOU WANT
WILL COME FROM THE MINORITY OF WHAT
YOU DO.

DATE:

TO-DO LIST	PARETO LIST	SUCCESS LIST
A long list of the things you think you need to do.	The most important 20 % from the to-do list.	The ONE THING you have to do.

TIME BLOCK:

From: _____ To: _____

Notes:

_____
_____
_____
_____
_____
_____
_____

THE MAJORITY OF WHAT YOU WANT
WILL COME FROM THE MINORITY OF WHAT
YOU DO.

DATE:

EFFORT

RESULT

DAYDREAMERS PRINT

DAILY SUCCESS LIST

UNTIL YOUR ONE THING IS DONE,
EVERYTHING ELSE IS A DISTRACTION!

TO-DO LIST	**PARETO LIST**	**SUCCESS LIST**
A long list of the things you think you need to do.	The most important 20 % from the to-do list.	The ONE THING you have to do.

TIME BLOCK:

From: _____ To: _____

Notes:

_____
_____
_____
_____
_____
_____
_____

THE MAJORITY OF WHAT YOU WANT
WILL COME FROM THE MINORITY OF WHAT
YOU DO.

DATE:

TO-DO LIST	**PARETO LIST**	**SUCCESS LIST**
A long list of the things you think you need to do.	The most important 20 % from the to-do list.	The ONE THING you have to do.

TIME BLOCK:

From: _____ To: _____

Notes:

_____
_____
_____
_____
_____
_____
_____

THE MAJORITY OF WHAT YOU WANT
WILL COME FROM THE MINORITY OF WHAT
YOU DO.

DATE:

  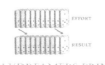

EFFORT

RESULT

DAILY SUCCESS LIST

UNTIL YOUR ONE THING IS DONE,
EVERYTHING ELSE IS A DISTRACTION!

TO-DO LIST	PARETO LIST	SUCCESS LIST
A long list of the things you think you need to do.	The most important 20 % from the to-do list.	The ONE THING you have to do.

TIME BLOCK:

From: _____ To: _____

Notes:

_____

_____

_____

_____

_____

_____

_____

THE MAJORITY OF WHAT YOU WANT WILL COME FROM THE MINORITY OF WHAT YOU DO.

DATE:

TO-DO LIST	PARETO LIST	SUCCESS LIST
A long list of the things you think you need to do.	The most important 20 % from the to-do list.	The ONE THING you have to do.

TIME BLOCK:

From: _____ To: _____

Notes:

_____

_____

_____

_____

_____

_____

_____

THE MAJORITY OF WHAT YOU WANT WILL COME FROM THE MINORITY OF WHAT YOU DO.

DATE:

DAYDREAMERS PRINT

DAILY SUCCESS LIST

UNTIL YOUR ONE THING IS DONE,
EVERYTHING ELSE IS A DISTRACTION!

TO-DO LIST	PARETO LIST	SUCCESS LIST
A long list of the things you think you need to do.	The most important 20 % from the to-do list.	The ONE THING you have to do.

TIME BLOCK:

From: _____ To: _____

Notes:

_____

_____

_____

_____

_____

_____

_____

THE MAJORITY OF WHAT YOU WANT
WILL COME FROM THE MINORITY OF WHAT
YOU DO.

DATE:

TO-DO LIST	PARETO LIST	SUCCESS LIST
A long list of the things you think you need to do.	The most important 20 % from the to-do list.	The ONE THING you have to do.

TIME BLOCK:

From: _____ To: _____

Notes:

_____

_____

_____

_____

_____

_____

_____

_____

THE MAJORITY OF WHAT YOU WANT
WILL COME FROM THE MINORITY OF WHAT
YOU DO.

DATE:

  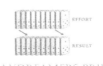

DAILY SUCCESS LIST

UNTIL YOUR ONE THING IS DONE,
EVERYTHING ELSE IS A DISTRACTION!

TO-DO LIST	**PARETO LIST**	**SUCCESS LIST**
A long list of the things you think you need to do.	The most important 20 % from the to-do list.	The ONE THING you have to do.

THE MAJORITY OF WHAT YOU WANT WILL COME FROM THE MINORITY OF WHAT YOU DO.

DATE:

TIME BLOCK:

From: _____ To: _____

Notes:

_____
_____
_____
_____
_____
_____
_____

TO-DO LIST	**PARETO LIST**	**SUCCESS LIST**
A long list of the things you think you need to do.	The most important 20 % from the to-do list.	The ONE THING you have to do.

THE MAJORITY OF WHAT YOU WANT WILL COME FROM THE MINORITY OF WHAT YOU DO.

DATE:

TIME BLOCK:

From: _____ To: _____

Notes:

_____
_____
_____
_____
_____
_____
_____

EFFORT

RESULT

DAYDREAMERS PRINT

DAILY SUCCESS LIST

UNTIL YOUR ONE THING IS DONE,
EVERYTHING ELSE IS A DISTRACTION!

TO-DO LIST	PARETO LIST	SUCCESS LIST
A long list of the things you think you need to do.	The most important 20 % from the to-do list.	The ONE THING you have to do.

TIME BLOCK:

From: _____ To: _____

Notes:

_____
_____
_____
_____
_____
_____
_____

THE MAJORITY OF WHAT YOU WANT
WILL COME FROM THE MINORITY OF WHAT
YOU DO.

DATE:

TO-DO LIST	PARETO LIST	SUCCESS LIST
A long list of the things you think you need to do.	The most important 20 % from the to-do list.	The ONE THING you have to do.

TIME BLOCK:

From: _____ To: _____

Notes:

_____
_____
_____
_____
_____
_____
_____

THE MAJORITY OF WHAT YOU WANT
WILL COME FROM THE MINORITY OF WHAT
YOU DO.

DATE:

  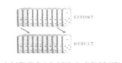

DAILY SUCCESS LIST

UNTIL YOUR ONE THING IS DONE,
EVERYTHING ELSE IS A DISTRACTION!

TO-DO LIST	PARETO LIST	SUCCESS LIST
A long list of the things you think you need to do.	The most important 20 % from the to-do list.	The ONE THING you have to do.

THE MAJORITY OF WHAT YOU WANT WILL COME FROM THE MINORITY OF WHAT YOU DO.

DATE:

TIME BLOCK:

From: _____ To: _____

Notes:

TO-DO LIST	PARETO LIST	SUCCESS LIST
A long list of the things you think you need to do.	The most important 20 % from the to-do list.	The ONE THING you have to do.

THE MAJORITY OF WHAT YOU WANT WILL COME FROM THE MINORITY OF WHAT YOU DO.

DATE:

TIME BLOCK:

From: _____ To: _____

Notes:

EFFORT

RESULT

DAILY SUCCESS LIST

UNTIL YOUR ONE THING IS DONE,
EVERYTHING ELSE IS A DISTRACTION!

TO-DO LIST	PARETO LIST	SUCCESS LIST
A long list of the things you think you need to do.	The most important 20 % from the to-do list.	The ONE THING you have to do.

TIME BLOCK:

From: _____ To: _____

Notes:

_____

_____

_____

_____

_____

_____

_____

THE MAJORITY OF WHAT YOU WANT
WILL COME FROM THE MINORITY OF WHAT
YOU DO.

DATE:

TO-DO LIST	PARETO LIST	SUCCESS LIST
A long list of the things you think you need to do.	The most important 20 % from the to-do list.	The ONE THING you have to do.

TIME BLOCK:

From: _____ To: _____

Notes:

_____

_____

_____

_____

_____

_____

_____

THE MAJORITY OF WHAT YOU WANT
WILL COME FROM THE MINORITY OF WHAT
YOU DO.

DATE:

  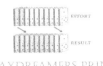 EFFORT / RESULT

DAILY SUCCESS LIST

UNTIL YOUR ONE THING IS DONE,
EVERYTHING ELSE IS A DISTRACTION!

TO-DO LIST	PARETO LIST	SUCCESS LIST
A long list of the things you think you need to do.	The most important 20 % from the to-do list.	The ONE THING you have to do.

THE MAJORITY OF WHAT YOU WANT WILL COME FROM THE MINORITY OF WHAT YOU DO.

DATE:

TIME BLOCK:

From: _____ To: _____

Notes:

_____

_____

_____

_____

_____

_____

TO-DO LIST	PARETO LIST	SUCCESS LIST
A long list of the things you think you need to do.	The most important 20 % from the to-do list.	The ONE THING you have to do.

THE MAJORITY OF WHAT YOU WANT WILL COME FROM THE MINORITY OF WHAT YOU DO.

DATE:

TIME BLOCK:

From: _____ To: _____

Notes:

_____

_____

_____

_____

_____

_____

_____

EFFORT

RESULT

DAYDREAMERS PRINT

DAILY SUCCESS LIST

UNTIL YOUR ONE THING IS DONE,
EVERYTHING ELSE IS A DISTRACTION!

TO-DO LIST	PARETO LIST	SUCCESS LIST
A long list of the things you think you need to do.	The most important 20 % from the to-do list.	The ONE THING you have to do.

TIME BLOCK:

From: _____ To: _____

Notes:

THE MAJORITY OF WHAT YOU WANT
WILL COME FROM THE MINORITY OF WHAT
YOU DO.

DATE:

TO-DO LIST	PARETO LIST	SUCCESS LIST
A long list of the things you think you need to do.	The most important 20 % from the to-do list.	The ONE THING you have to do.

TIME BLOCK:

From: _____ To: _____

Notes:

THE MAJORITY OF WHAT YOU WANT
WILL COME FROM THE MINORITY OF WHAT
YOU DO.

DATE:

  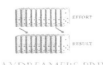 

DAILY SUCCESS LIST

UNTIL YOUR ONE THING IS DONE,
EVERYTHING ELSE IS A DISTRACTION!

TO-DO LIST	PARETO LIST	SUCCESS LIST
A long list of the things you think you need to do.	The most important 20 % from the to-do list.	The ONE THING you have to do.

TIME BLOCK:

From: _____ To: _____

Notes:

_____
_____
_____
_____
_____
_____
_____

THE MAJORITY OF WHAT YOU WANT
WILL COME FROM THE MINORITY OF WHAT
YOU DO.

DATE:

TO-DO LIST	PARETO LIST	SUCCESS LIST
A long list of the things you think you need to do.	The most important 20 % from the to-do list.	The ONE THING you have to do.

TIME BLOCK:

From: _____ To: _____

Notes:

_____
_____
_____
_____
_____
_____
_____

THE MAJORITY OF WHAT YOU WANT
WILL COME FROM THE MINORITY OF WHAT
YOU DO.

DATE:

EFFORT

RESULT

DAYDREAMERS PRINT

DAILY SUCCESS LIST

UNTIL YOUR ONE THING IS DONE,
EVERYTHING ELSE IS A DISTRACTION!

TO-DO LIST	PARETO LIST	SUCCESS LIST
A long list of the things you think you need to do.	The most important 20 % from the to-do list.	The ONE THING you have to do.

TIME BLOCK:

From: _____ To: _____

Notes:

_____
_____
_____
_____
_____
_____
_____

THE MAJORITY OF WHAT YOU WANT
WILL COME FROM THE MINORITY OF WHAT
YOU DO.

DATE:

TO-DO LIST	PARETO LIST	SUCCESS LIST
A long list of the things you think you need to do.	The most important 20 % from the to-do list.	The ONE THING you have to do.

TIME BLOCK:

From: _____ To: _____

Notes:

_____
_____
_____
_____
_____
_____

THE MAJORITY OF WHAT YOU WANT
WILL COME FROM THE MINORITY OF WHAT
YOU DO.

DATE:

  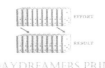

EFFORT

RESULT

DAYDREAMERS PRINT

DAILY SUCCESS LIST

UNTIL YOUR ONE THING IS DONE,
EVERYTHING ELSE IS A DISTRACTION!

TO-DO LIST	PARETO LIST	SUCCESS LIST
A long list of the things you think you need to do.	The most important 20 % from the to-do list.	The ONE THING you have to do.

TIME BLOCK:

From: _____ To: _____

Notes:

_____
_____
_____
_____
_____

THE MAJORITY OF WHAT YOU WANT
WILL COME FROM THE MINORITY OF WHAT
YOU DO.

DATE:

TO-DO LIST	PARETO LIST	SUCCESS LIST
A long list of the things you think you need to do.	The most important 20 % from the to-do list.	The ONE THING you have to do.

TIME BLOCK:

From: _____ To: _____

Notes:

_____
_____
_____
_____
_____

THE MAJORITY OF WHAT YOU WANT
WILL COME FROM THE MINORITY OF WHAT
YOU DO.

DATE:

EFFORT

RESULT

DAYDREAMERS PRINT

DAILY SUCCESS LIST

UNTIL YOUR ONE THING IS DONE,
EVERYTHING ELSE IS A DISTRACTION!

TO-DO LIST	PARETO LIST	SUCCESS LIST
A long list of the things you think you need to do.	The most important 20 % from the to-do list.	The ONE THING you have to do.

TIME BLOCK:

From: _____ To: _____

Notes:

_____
_____
_____
_____
_____
_____
_____

THE MAJORITY OF WHAT YOU WANT
WILL COME FROM THE MINORITY OF WHAT
YOU DO.

DATE:

TO-DO LIST	PARETO LIST	SUCCESS LIST
A long list of the things you think you need to do.	The most important 20 % from the to-do list.	The ONE THING you have to do.

TIME BLOCK:

From: _____ To: _____

Notes:

_____
_____
_____
_____
_____
_____
_____

THE MAJORITY OF WHAT YOU WANT
WILL COME FROM THE MINORITY OF WHAT
YOU DO.

DATE:

  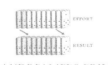

DAILY SUCCESS LIST

UNTIL YOUR ONE THING IS DONE,
EVERYTHING ELSE IS A DISTRACTION!

TO-DO LIST	PARETO LIST	SUCCESS LIST
A long list of the things you think you need to do.	The most important 20 % from the to-do list.	The ONE THING you have to do.

TIME BLOCK:

From: _____ To: _____

Notes:

_____

_____

_____

_____

_____

_____

_____

THE MAJORITY OF WHAT YOU WANT
WILL COME FROM THE MINORITY OF WHAT
YOU DO.

DATE:

TO-DO LIST	PARETO LIST	SUCCESS LIST
A long list of the things you think you need to do.	The most important 20 % from the to-do list.	The ONE THING you have to do.

TIME BLOCK:

From: _____ To: _____

Notes:

_____

_____

_____

_____

_____

_____

_____

THE MAJORITY OF WHAT YOU WANT
WILL COME FROM THE MINORITY OF WHAT
YOU DO.

DATE:

DAILY SUCCESS LIST

UNTIL YOUR ONE THING IS DONE,
EVERYTHING ELSE IS A DISTRACTION!

TO-DO LIST	PARETO LIST	SUCCESS LIST
A long list of the things you think you need to do.	The most important 20 % from the to-do list.	The ONE THING you have to do.

TIME BLOCK:

From: _____ To: _____

Notes:

_____

_____

_____

_____

_____

_____

_____

THE MAJORITY OF WHAT YOU WANT
WILL COME FROM THE MINORITY OF WHAT
YOU DO.

DATE:

TO-DO LIST	PARETO LIST	SUCCESS LIST
A long list of the things you think you need to do.	The most important 20 % from the to-do list.	The ONE THING you have to do.

TIME BLOCK:

From: _____ To: _____

Notes:

_____

_____

_____

_____

_____

_____

_____

THE MAJORITY OF WHAT YOU WANT
WILL COME FROM THE MINORITY OF WHAT
YOU DO.

DATE:

  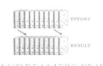 EFFORT RESULT

DAILY SUCCESS LIST

UNTIL YOUR ONE THING IS DONE,
EVERYTHING ELSE IS A DISTRACTION!

TO-DO LIST
A long list of the things you think you need to do.

PARETO LIST
The most important 20 % from the to-do list.

SUCCESS LIST
The ONE THING you have to do.

THE MAJORITY OF WHAT YOU WANT WILL COME FROM THE MINORITY OF WHAT YOU DO.

DATE:

TIME BLOCK:

From: _____ To: _____

Notes:

_____
_____
_____
_____
_____
_____

TO-DO LIST
A long list of the things you think you need to do.

PARETO LIST
The most important 20 % from the to-do list.

SUCCESS LIST
The ONE THING you have to do.

THE MAJORITY OF WHAT YOU WANT WILL COME FROM THE MINORITY OF WHAT YOU DO.

DATE:

TIME BLOCK:

From: _____ To: _____

Notes:

_____
_____
_____
_____
_____
_____

EFFORT

RESULT

DAYDREAMERS PRINT

DAILY SUCCESS LIST

UNTIL YOUR ONE THING IS DONE,
EVERYTHING ELSE IS A DISTRACTION!

TO-DO LIST	PARETO LIST	SUCCESS LIST
A long list of the things you think you need to do.	The most important 20 % from the to-do list.	The ONE THING you have to do.

TIME BLOCK:

From: _____ To: _____

Notes:

THE MAJORITY OF WHAT YOU WANT
WILL COME FROM THE MINORITY OF WHAT
YOU DO.

DATE:

TO-DO LIST	PARETO LIST	SUCCESS LIST
A long list of the things you think you need to do.	The most important 20 % from the to-do list.	The ONE THING you have to do.

TIME BLOCK:

From: _____ To: _____

Notes:

THE MAJORITY OF WHAT YOU WANT
WILL COME FROM THE MINORITY OF WHAT
YOU DO.

DATE:

  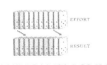

DAILY SUCCESS LIST

UNTIL YOUR ONE THING IS DONE,
EVERYTHING ELSE IS A DISTRACTION!

TO-DO LIST	PARETO LIST	SUCCESS LIST
A long list of the things you think you need to do.	The most important 20 % from the to-do list.	The ONE THING you have to do.

TIME BLOCK:

From: _____ To: _____

Notes:

_____

_____

_____

_____

_____

_____

THE MAJORITY OF WHAT YOU WANT
WILL COME FROM THE MINORITY OF WHAT
YOU DO.

DATE:

TO-DO LIST	PARETO LIST	SUCCESS LIST
A long list of the things you think you need to do.	The most important 20 % from the to-do list.	The ONE THING you have to do.

TIME BLOCK:

From: _____ To: _____

Notes:

_____

_____

_____

_____

_____

_____

THE MAJORITY OF WHAT YOU WANT
WILL COME FROM THE MINORITY OF WHAT
YOU DO.

DATE:

DAILY SUCCESS LIST

UNTIL YOUR ONE THING IS DONE,
EVERYTHING ELSE IS A DISTRACTION!

TO-DO LIST
A long list of the things you think you need to do.

PARETO LIST
The most important 20 % from the to-do list.

SUCCESS LIST
The ONE THING you have to do.

THE MAJORITY OF WHAT YOU WANT
WILL COME FROM THE MINORITY OF WHAT
YOU DO.

DATE:

TIME BLOCK:

From: _____ To: _____

Notes:

_____

_____

_____

_____

_____

_____

_____

_____

TO-DO LIST
A long list of the things you think you need to do.

PARETO LIST
The most important 20 % from the to-do list.

SUCCESS LIST
The ONE THING you have to do.

THE MAJORITY OF WHAT YOU WANT
WILL COME FROM THE MINORITY OF WHAT
YOU DO.

DATE:

TIME BLOCK:

From: _____ To: _____

Notes:

_____

_____

_____

_____

_____

_____

_____

_____

  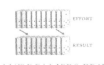 

EFFORT

RESULT

DAYDREAMERS PRINT

DAILY SUCCESS LIST

UNTIL YOUR ONE THING IS DONE,
EVERYTHING ELSE IS A DISTRACTION!

TO-DO LIST	PARETO LIST	SUCCESS LIST
A long list of the things you think you need to do.	The most important 20 % from the to-do list.	The ONE THING you have to do.

TIME BLOCK:

From: _____ To: _____

Notes:

_____

_____

_____

_____

_____

_____

THE MAJORITY OF WHAT YOU WANT
WILL COME FROM THE MINORITY OF WHAT
YOU DO.

DATE:

TO-DO LIST	PARETO LIST	SUCCESS LIST
A long list of the things you think you need to do.	The most important 20 % from the to-do list.	The ONE THING you have to do.

TIME BLOCK:

From: _____ To: _____

Notes:

_____

_____

_____

_____

_____

_____

_____

_____

THE MAJORITY OF WHAT YOU WANT
WILL COME FROM THE MINORITY OF WHAT
YOU DO.

DATE:

DAYDREAMERS PRINT

DAILY SUCCESS LIST

UNTIL YOUR ONE THING IS DONE,
EVERYTHING ELSE IS A DISTRACTION!

TO-DO LIST	PARETO LIST	SUCCESS LIST
A long list of the things you think you need to do.	The most important 20 % from the to-do list.	The ONE THING you have to do.

TIME BLOCK:

From: _____ To: _____

Notes:

_____
_____
_____
_____
_____
_____
_____

THE MAJORITY OF WHAT YOU WANT
WILL COME FROM THE MINORITY OF WHAT
YOU DO.

DATE:

TO-DO LIST	PARETO LIST	SUCCESS LIST
A long list of the things you think you need to do.	The most important 20 % from the to-do list.	The ONE THING you have to do.

TIME BLOCK:

From: _____ To: _____

Notes:

_____
_____
_____
_____
_____
_____
_____

THE MAJORITY OF WHAT YOU WANT
WILL COME FROM THE MINORITY OF WHAT
YOU DO.

DATE:

  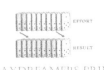

DAILY SUCCESS LIST

UNTIL YOUR ONE THING IS DONE,
EVERYTHING ELSE IS A DISTRACTION!

TO-DO LIST
A long list of the things you think you need to do.

PARETO LIST
The most important 20 % from the to-do list.

THE MAJORITY OF WHAT YOU WANT
WILL COME FROM THE MINORITY OF WHAT
YOU DO.

DATE:

SUCCESS LIST
The ONE THING you have to do.

TIME BLOCK:

From: _____ To: _____

Notes:

_____
_____
_____
_____
_____
_____
_____

TO-DO LIST
A long list of the things you think you need to do.

PARETO LIST
The most important 20 % from the to-do list.

THE MAJORITY OF WHAT YOU WANT
WILL COME FROM THE MINORITY OF WHAT
YOU DO.

DATE:

SUCCESS LIST
The ONE THING you have to do.

TIME BLOCK:

From: _____ To: _____

Notes:

_____
_____
_____
_____
_____
_____
_____

DAYDREAMERS PRINT

DAILY SUCCESS LIST

UNTIL YOUR ONE THING IS DONE,
EVERYTHING ELSE IS A DISTRACTION!

TO-DO LIST	PARETO LIST	SUCCESS LIST
A long list of the things you think you need to do.	The most important 20 % from the to-do list.	The ONE THING you have to do.

TIME BLOCK:

From: _____ To: _____

Notes:

_____

THE MAJORITY OF WHAT YOU WANT
WILL COME FROM THE MINORITY OF WHAT
YOU DO.

DATE:

TO-DO LIST	PARETO LIST	SUCCESS LIST
A long list of the things you think you need to do.	The most important 20 % from the to-do list.	The ONE THING you have to do.

TIME BLOCK:

From: _____ To: _____

Notes:

_____

THE MAJORITY OF WHAT YOU WANT
WILL COME FROM THE MINORITY OF WHAT
YOU DO.

DATE:

  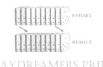

EFFORT

RESULT

DAILY SUCCESS LIST

UNTIL YOUR ONE THING IS DONE,
EVERYTHING ELSE IS A DISTRACTION!

TO-DO LIST	PARETO LIST	SUCCESS LIST
A long list of the things you think you need to do.	The most important 20 % from the to-do list.	The ONE THING you have to do.

PARETO LIST

THE MAJORITY OF WHAT YOU WANT WILL COME FROM THE MINORITY OF WHAT YOU DO.

DATE:

SUCCESS LIST

TIME BLOCK:

From: _____ To: _____

Notes:

_____
_____
_____
_____
_____
_____
_____
_____

TO-DO LIST	PARETO LIST	SUCCESS LIST
A long list of the things you think you need to do.	The most important 20 % from the to-do list.	The ONE THING you have to do.

THE MAJORITY OF WHAT YOU WANT WILL COME FROM THE MINORITY OF WHAT YOU DO.

DATE:

TIME BLOCK:

From: _____ To: _____

Notes:

_____
_____
_____
_____
_____
_____
_____
_____

EFFORT

RESULT

DAYDREAMERS PRINT

DAILY SUCCESS LIST

UNTIL YOUR ONE THING IS DONE,
EVERYTHING ELSE IS A DISTRACTION!

TO-DO LIST	PARETO LIST	SUCCESS LIST
A long list of the things you think you need to do.	The most important 20 % from the to-do list.	The ONE THING you have to do.

TIME BLOCK:

From: _____ To: _____

Notes:

_____
_____
_____
_____
_____
_____

THE MAJORITY OF WHAT YOU WANT
WILL COME FROM THE MINORITY OF WHAT
YOU DO.

DATE:

TO-DO LIST	PARETO LIST	SUCCESS LIST
A long list of the things you think you need to do.	The most important 20 % from the to-do list.	The ONE THING you have to do.

TIME BLOCK:

From: _____ To: _____

Notes:

_____
_____
_____
_____
_____
_____

THE MAJORITY OF WHAT YOU WANT
WILL COME FROM THE MINORITY OF WHAT
YOU DO.

DATE:

  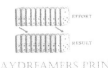

DAILY SUCCESS LIST

UNTIL YOUR ONE THING IS DONE,
EVERYTHING ELSE IS A DISTRACTION!

TO-DO LIST	PARETO LIST	SUCCESS LIST
A long list of the things you think you need to do.	The most important 20 % from the to-do list.	The ONE THING you have to do.

TIME BLOCK:

From: _____ To: _____

Notes:

_____
_____
_____
_____
_____
_____
_____

THE MAJORITY OF WHAT YOU WANT WILL COME FROM THE MINORITY OF WHAT YOU DO.

DATE:

TO-DO LIST	PARETO LIST	SUCCESS LIST
A long list of the things you think you need to do.	The most important 20 % from the to-do list.	The ONE THING you have to do.

TIME BLOCK:

From: _____ To: _____

Notes:

_____
_____
_____
_____
_____
_____
_____

THE MAJORITY OF WHAT YOU WANT WILL COME FROM THE MINORITY OF WHAT YOU DO.

DATE:

DAILY SUCCESS LIST

UNTIL YOUR ONE THING IS DONE,
EVERYTHING ELSE IS A DISTRACTION!

TO-DO LIST	PARETO LIST	SUCCESS LIST
A long list of the things you think you need to do.	The most important 20 % from the to-do list.	The ONE THING you have to do.

TIME BLOCK:

From: _____ To: _____

Notes:

_____

_____

_____

_____

_____

_____

_____

THE MAJORITY OF WHAT YOU WANT
WILL COME FROM THE MINORITY OF WHAT
YOU DO.

DATE:

TO-DO LIST	PARETO LIST	SUCCESS LIST
A long list of the things you think you need to do.	The most important 20 % from the to-do list.	The ONE THING you have to do.

TIME BLOCK:

From: _____ To: _____

Notes:

_____

_____

_____

_____

_____

_____

_____

THE MAJORITY OF WHAT YOU WANT
WILL COME FROM THE MINORITY OF WHAT
YOU DO.

DATE:

  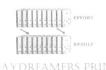

EFFORT

RESULT

DAYDREAMERS PRINT

DAILY SUCCESS LIST

UNTIL YOUR ONE THING IS DONE,
EVERYTHING ELSE IS A DISTRACTION!

TO-DO LIST	PARETO LIST	SUCCESS LIST
A long list of the things you think you need to do.	The most important 20 % from the to-do list.	The ONE THING you have to do.

THE MAJORITY OF WHAT YOU WANT WILL COME FROM THE MINORITY OF WHAT YOU DO.

DATE:

TIME BLOCK:

From: _____ To: _____

Notes:

_____

TO-DO LIST	PARETO LIST	SUCCESS LIST
A long list of the things you think you need to do.	The most important 20 % from the to-do list.	The ONE THING you have to do.

THE MAJORITY OF WHAT YOU WANT WILL COME FROM THE MINORITY OF WHAT YOU DO.

DATE:

TIME BLOCK:

From: _____ To: _____

Notes:

_____

EFFORT

RESULT

DAILY SUCCESS LIST

UNTIL YOUR ONE THING IS DONE,
EVERYTHING ELSE IS A DISTRACTION!

TO-DO LIST	PARETO LIST	SUCCESS LIST
A long list of the things you think you need to do.	The most important 20 % from the to-do list.	The ONE THING you have to do.

TIME BLOCK:

From: _____ To: _____

Notes:

THE MAJORITY OF WHAT YOU WANT
WILL COME FROM THE MINORITY OF WHAT
YOU DO.

DATE:

TO-DO LIST	PARETO LIST	SUCCESS LIST
A long list of the things you think you need to do.	The most important 20 % from the to-do list.	The ONE THING you have to do.

TIME BLOCK:

From: _____ To: _____

Notes:

THE MAJORITY OF WHAT YOU WANT
WILL COME FROM THE MINORITY OF WHAT
YOU DO.

DATE:

  EFFORT RESULT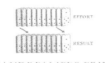

DAYDREAMERS PRINT

DAILY SUCCESS LIST

UNTIL YOUR ONE THING IS DONE,
EVERYTHING ELSE IS A DISTRACTION!

TO-DO LIST	PARETO LIST	SUCCESS LIST
A long list of the things you think you need to do.	The most important 20 % from the to-do list.	The ONE THING you have to do.

THE MAJORITY OF WHAT YOU WANT WILL COME FROM THE MINORITY OF WHAT YOU DO.

DATE:

TIME BLOCK:

From: _____ To: _____

Notes:

TO-DO LIST	PARETO LIST	SUCCESS LIST
A long list of the things you think you need to do.	The most important 20 % from the to-do list.	The ONE THING you have to do.

THE MAJORITY OF WHAT YOU WANT WILL COME FROM THE MINORITY OF WHAT YOU DO.

DATE:

TIME BLOCK:

From: _____ To: _____

Notes:

EFFORT

RESULT

DAYDREAMERS PRINT

DAILY SUCCESS LIST

UNTIL YOUR ONE THING IS DONE,
EVERYTHING ELSE IS A DISTRACTION!

TO-DO LIST	PARETO LIST	SUCCESS LIST
A long list of the things you think you need to do.	The most important 20 % from the to-do list.	The ONE THING you have to do.

TIME BLOCK:

From: _____ To: _____

Notes:

_____

_____

_____

_____

_____

_____

THE MAJORITY OF WHAT YOU WANT
WILL COME FROM THE MINORITY OF WHAT
YOU DO.

DATE:

TO-DO LIST	PARETO LIST	SUCCESS LIST
A long list of the things you think you need to do.	The most important 20 % from the to-do list.	The ONE THING you have to do.

TIME BLOCK:

From: _____ To: _____

Notes:

_____

_____

_____

_____

_____

_____

THE MAJORITY OF WHAT YOU WANT
WILL COME FROM THE MINORITY OF WHAT
YOU DO.

DATE:

  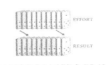

DAILY SUCCESS LIST

UNTIL YOUR ONE THING IS DONE,
EVERYTHING ELSE IS A DISTRACTION!

TO-DO LIST	**PARETO LIST**	**SUCCESS LIST**
A long list of the things you think you need to do.	The most important 20 % from the to-do list.	The ONE THING you have to do.

THE MAJORITY OF WHAT YOU WANT WILL COME FROM THE MINORITY OF WHAT YOU DO.

DATE:

TIME BLOCK:

From: _____ To: _____

Notes:

_____

_____

_____

_____

_____

_____

_____

TO-DO LIST	**PARETO LIST**	**SUCCESS LIST**
A long list of the things you think you need to do.	The most important 20 % from the to-do list.	The ONE THING you have to do.

THE MAJORITY OF WHAT YOU WANT WILL COME FROM THE MINORITY OF WHAT YOU DO.

DATE:

TIME BLOCK:

From: _____ To: _____

Notes:

_____

_____

_____

_____

_____

_____

_____

EFFORT

RESULT

DAYDREAMERS PRINT

DAILY SUCCESS LIST

UNTIL YOUR ONE THING IS DONE,
EVERYTHING ELSE IS A DISTRACTION!

TO-DO LIST	PARETO LIST	SUCCESS LIST
A long list of the things you think you need to do.	The most important 20 % from the to-do list.	The ONE THING you have to do.

TIME BLOCK:

From: _____ To: _____

Notes:

_____
_____
_____
_____
_____
_____
_____

THE MAJORITY OF WHAT YOU WANT WILL COME FROM THE MINORITY OF WHAT YOU DO.

DATE:

TO-DO LIST	PARETO LIST	SUCCESS LIST
A long list of the things you think you need to do.	The most important 20 % from the to-do list.	The ONE THING you have to do.

TIME BLOCK:

From: _____ To: _____

Notes:

_____
_____
_____
_____
_____
_____
_____

THE MAJORITY OF WHAT YOU WANT WILL COME FROM THE MINORITY OF WHAT YOU DO.

DATE:

  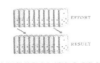

DAYDREAMERS PRINT

DAILY SUCCESS LIST

UNTIL YOUR ONE THING IS DONE,
EVERYTHING ELSE IS A DISTRACTION!

TO-DO LIST	PARETO LIST	SUCCESS LIST
A long list of the things you think you need to do.	The most important 20 % from the to-do list.	The ONE THING you have to do.

THE MAJORITY OF WHAT YOU WANT WILL COME FROM THE MINORITY OF WHAT YOU DO.

DATE:

TIME BLOCK:

From: _____ To: _____

Notes:

TO-DO LIST	PARETO LIST	SUCCESS LIST
A long list of the things you think you need to do.	The most important 20 % from the to-do list.	The ONE THING you have to do.

THE MAJORITY OF WHAT YOU WANT WILL COME FROM THE MINORITY OF WHAT YOU DO.

DATE:

TIME BLOCK:

From: _____ To: _____

Notes:

  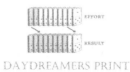 

EFFORT

RESULT

DAYDREAMERS PRINT

DAILY SUCCESS LIST

UNTIL YOUR ONE THING IS DONE,
EVERYTHING ELSE IS A DISTRACTION!

TO-DO LIST	PARETO LIST	SUCCESS LIST
A long list of the things you think you need to do.	The most important 20 % from the to-do list.	The ONE THING you have to do.

THE MAJORITY OF WHAT YOU WANT WILL COME FROM THE MINORITY OF WHAT YOU DO.

DATE:

TIME BLOCK:

From: _____ To: _____

Notes:

TO-DO LIST	PARETO LIST	SUCCESS LIST
A long list of the things you think you need to do.	The most important 20 % from the to-do list.	The ONE THING you have to do.

THE MAJORITY OF WHAT YOU WANT WILL COME FROM THE MINORITY OF WHAT YOU DO.

DATE:

TIME BLOCK:

From: _____ To: _____

Notes:

EFFORT

RESULT

DAILY SUCCESS LIST

UNTIL YOUR ONE THING IS DONE,
EVERYTHING ELSE IS A DISTRACTION!

TO-DO LIST	PARETO LIST	SUCCESS LIST
A long list of the things you think you need to do.	The most important 20 % from the to-do list.	The ONE THING you have to do.

TIME BLOCK:

From: _____ To: _____

Notes:

_____

_____

_____

_____

_____

_____

THE MAJORITY OF WHAT YOU WANT
WILL COME FROM THE MINORITY OF WHAT
YOU DO.

DATE:

TO-DO LIST	PARETO LIST	SUCCESS LIST
A long list of the things you think you need to do.	The most important 20 % from the to-do list.	The ONE THING you have to do.

TIME BLOCK:

From: _____ To: _____

Notes:

_____

_____

_____

_____

_____

_____

THE MAJORITY OF WHAT YOU WANT
WILL COME FROM THE MINORITY OF WHAT
YOU DO.

DATE:

DAYDREAMERS PRINT

DAILY SUCCESS LIST

UNTIL YOUR ONE THING IS DONE,
EVERYTHING ELSE IS A DISTRACTION!

TO-DO LIST	PARETO LIST	SUCCESS LIST
A long list of the things you think you need to do.	The most important 20 % from the to-do list.	The ONE THING you have to do.

TIME BLOCK:

From: _____ To: _____

Notes:

_____
_____
_____
_____
_____
_____
_____
_____

THE MAJORITY OF WHAT YOU WANT
WILL COME FROM THE MINORITY OF WHAT
YOU DO.

DATE:

TO-DO LIST	PARETO LIST	SUCCESS LIST
A long list of the things you think you need to do.	The most important 20 % from the to-do list.	The ONE THING you have to do.

TIME BLOCK:

From: _____ To: _____

Notes:

_____
_____
_____
_____
_____
_____
_____
_____

THE MAJORITY OF WHAT YOU WANT
WILL COME FROM THE MINORITY OF WHAT
YOU DO.

DATE:

  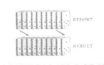

EFFORT

RESULT

DAYDREAMERS PRINT

DAILY SUCCESS LIST

UNTIL YOUR ONE THING IS DONE,
EVERYTHING ELSE IS A DISTRACTION!

TO-DO LIST	PARETO LIST	SUCCESS LIST
A long list of the things you think you need to do.	The most important 20 % from the to-do list.	The ONE THING you have to do.

TIME BLOCK:

From: _____ To: _____

Notes:

_____

_____

_____

_____

_____

_____

_____

_____

THE MAJORITY OF WHAT YOU WANT
WILL COME FROM THE MINORITY OF WHAT
YOU DO.

DATE:

TO-DO LIST	PARETO LIST	SUCCESS LIST
A long list of the things you think you need to do.	The most important 20 % from the to-do list.	The ONE THING you have to do.

TIME BLOCK:

From: _____ To: _____

Notes:

_____

_____

_____

_____

_____

_____

_____

_____

THE MAJORITY OF WHAT YOU WANT
WILL COME FROM THE MINORITY OF WHAT
YOU DO.

DATE:

EFFORT

RESULT

DAYDREAMERS PRINT

DAILY SUCCESS LIST

UNTIL YOUR ONE THING IS DONE,
EVERYTHING ELSE IS A DISTRACTION!

TO-DO LIST	PARETO LIST	SUCCESS LIST
A long list of the things you think you need to do.	The most important 20 % from the to-do list.	The ONE THING you have to do.

TIME BLOCK:

From: _____ To: _____

Notes:

_____

THE MAJORITY OF WHAT YOU WANT
WILL COME FROM THE MINORITY OF WHAT
YOU DO.

DATE:

TO-DO LIST	PARETO LIST	SUCCESS LIST
A long list of the things you think you need to do.	The most important 20 % from the to-do list.	The ONE THING you have to do.

TIME BLOCK:

From: _____ To: _____

Notes:

_____

THE MAJORITY OF WHAT YOU WANT
WILL COME FROM THE MINORITY OF WHAT
YOU DO.

DATE:

  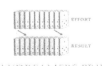

DAILY SUCCESS LIST

UNTIL YOUR ONE THING IS DONE,
EVERYTHING ELSE IS A DISTRACTION!

TO-DO LIST	PARETO LIST	SUCCESS LIST
A long list of the things you think you need to do.	The most important 20 % from the to-do list.	The ONE THING you have to do.

TIME BLOCK:

From: _____ To: _____

Notes:

_____

THE MAJORITY OF WHAT YOU WANT WILL COME FROM THE MINORITY OF WHAT YOU DO.

DATE:

TO-DO LIST	PARETO LIST	SUCCESS LIST
A long list of the things you think you need to do.	The most important 20 % from the to-do list.	The ONE THING you have to do.

TIME BLOCK:

From: _____ To: _____

Notes:

_____

THE MAJORITY OF WHAT YOU WANT WILL COME FROM THE MINORITY OF WHAT YOU DO.

DATE:

DAYDREAMERS PRINT

DAILY SUCCESS LIST

UNTIL YOUR ONE THING IS DONE,
EVERYTHING ELSE IS A DISTRACTION!

TO-DO LIST	PARETO LIST	SUCCESS LIST
A long list of the things you think you need to do.	The most important 20 % from the to-do list.	The ONE THING you have to do.

TIME BLOCK:

From: _____ To: _____

Notes:

_____

_____

_____

_____

_____

_____

_____

THE MAJORITY OF WHAT YOU WANT
WILL COME FROM THE MINORITY OF WHAT
YOU DO.

DATE:

TO-DO LIST	PARETO LIST	SUCCESS LIST
A long list of the things you think you need to do.	The most important 20 % from the to-do list.	The ONE THING you have to do.

TIME BLOCK:

From: _____ To: _____

Notes:

_____

_____

_____

_____

_____

_____

_____

THE MAJORITY OF WHAT YOU WANT
WILL COME FROM THE MINORITY OF WHAT
YOU DO.

DATE:

  EFFORT RESULT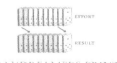

DAYDREAMERS PRINT

DAILY SUCCESS LIST

UNTIL YOUR ONE THING IS DONE,
EVERYTHING ELSE IS A DISTRACTION!

TO-DO LIST
A long list of the things you think you need to do.

PARETO LIST
The most important 20 % from the to-do list.

SUCCESS LIST
The ONE THING you have to do.

TIME BLOCK:

From: _____ To: _____

Notes:

_____

_____

_____

_____

_____

_____

THE MAJORITY OF WHAT YOU WANT
WILL COME FROM THE MINORITY OF WHAT
YOU DO.

DATE:

TO-DO LIST
A long list of the things you think you need to do.

PARETO LIST
The most important 20 % from the to-do list.

SUCCESS LIST
The ONE THING you have to do.

TIME BLOCK:

From: _____ To: _____

Notes:

_____

_____

_____

_____

_____

_____

THE MAJORITY OF WHAT YOU WANT
WILL COME FROM THE MINORITY OF WHAT
YOU DO.

DATE:

EFFORT

RESULT

DAYDREAMERS PRINT

GOAL SETTING TO THE NOW

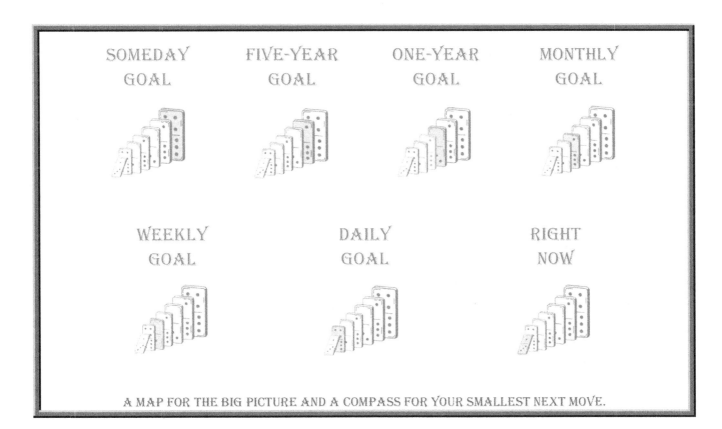

SOMEDAY GOAL FIVE-YEAR GOAL ONE-YEAR GOAL MONTHLY GOAL

WEEKLY GOAL DAILY GOAL RIGHT NOW

A MAP FOR THE BIG PICTURE AND A COMPASS FOR YOUR SMALLEST NEXT MOVE.

GOAL SETTING TO THE NOW

A MAP FOR THE BIG PICTURE AND A COMPASS FOR YOUR SMALLEST NEXT MOVE.

SOMEDAY GOAL

What's the **ONE THING** I want to do **someday**? What's the **ONE THING** I can do in my life that would **mean the most to me and the world**, such that by doing it everything else would be easier or unnecessary?

FIVE-YEAR GOAL

Based on my Someday goal, what's the **ONE THING** I can do in **the next five years,** such that doing it everything else will be easier or unnecessary?

ONE-YEAR GOAL

Based on my Five-year goal, what's the **ONE THING** I can do **this year,** such that doing it everything else will be easier or unnecessary?

MONTHLY GOAL

Based on my One-year goal, what's the **ONE THING** I can do **this month,** such that doing it everything else will be easier or unnecessary?

WEEKLY GOAL

Based on my Monthly goal, what's the **ONE THING** I can do **this week,** such that doing it everything else will be easier or unnecessary?

DAILY GOAL

Based on my Weekly goal, what's the **ONE THING** I can do **today,** such that doing it everything else will be easier or unnecessary?

RIGHT NOW

Based on my Daily goal, what's the **ONE THING** I can do **right now,** such that doing it everything else will be easier or unnecessary?

GOAL SETTING TO THE NOW

A MAP FOR THE BIG PICTURE AND A COMPASS FOR YOUR SMALLEST NEXT MOVE.

SOMEDAY GOAL

What's the **ONE THING** I want to do **someday**? What's the **ONE THING** I can do in my life that would **mean the most to me and the world**, such that by doing it everything else would be easier or unnecessary?

FIVE-YEAR GOAL

Based on my Someday goal, what's the **ONE THING** I can do **in the next five years,** such that doing it everything else will be easier or unnecessary?

ONE-YEAR GOAL

Based on my Five-year goal, what's the **ONE THING** I can do **this year,** such that doing it everything else will be easier or unnecessary?

MONTHLY GOAL

Based on my One-year goal, what's the **ONE THING** I can do **this month,** such that doing it everything else will be easier or unnecessary?

WEEKLY GOAL

Based on my Monthly goal, what's the **ONE THING** I can do **this week,** such that doing it everything else will be easier or unnecessary?

DAILY GOAL

Based on my Weekly goal, what's the **ONE THING** I can do **today,** such that doing it everything else will be easier or unnecessary?

RIGHT NOW

Based on my Daily goal, what's the **ONE THING** I can do **right now,** such that doing it everything else will be easier or unnecessary?

GOAL SETTING TO THE NOW

A MAP FOR THE BIG PICTURE AND A COMPASS FOR YOUR SMALLEST NEXT MOVE.

SOMEDAY GOAL

What's the **ONE THING** I want to do **someday**? What's the **ONE THING** I can do in my life that would **mean the most to me and the world**, such that by doing it everything else would be easier or unnecessary?

FIVE-YEAR GOAL

Based on my Someday goal, what's the **ONE THING** I can do in **the next five years,** such that doing it everything else will be easier or unnecessary?

ONE-YEAR GOAL

Based on my Five-year goal, what's the **ONE THING** I can do **this year,** such that doing it everything else will be easier or unnecessary?

MONTHLY GOAL

Based on my One-year goal, what's the **ONE THING** I can do **this month,** such that doing it everything else will be easier or unnecessary?

WEEKLY GOAL

Based on my Monthly goal, what's the **ONE THING** I can do **this week,** such that doing it everything else will be easier or unnecessary?

DAILY GOAL

Based on my Weekly goal, what's the **ONE THING** I can do **today,** such that doing it everything else will be easier or unnecessary?

RIGHT NOW

Based on my Daily goal, what's the **ONE THING** I can do **right now,** such that doing it everything else will be easier or unnecessary?

GOAL SETTING TO THE NOW

A MAP FOR THE BIG PICTURE AND A COMPASS FOR YOUR SMALLEST NEXT MOVE.

SOMEDAY GOAL

What's the **ONE THING** I want to do **someday**? What's the **ONE THING** I can do in my life that would **mean the most to me and the world**, such that by doing it everything else would be easier or unnecessary?

FIVE-YEAR GOAL

Based on my Someday goal, what's the **ONE THING** I can do in **the next five years,** such that doing it everything else will be easier or unnecessary?

ONE-YEAR GOAL

Based on my Five-year goal, what's the **ONE THING** I can do **this year,** such that doing it everything else will be easier or unnecessary?

MONTHLY GOAL

Based on my One-year goal, what's the **ONE THING** I can do **this month,** such that doing it everything else will be easier or unnecessary?

WEEKLY GOAL

Based on my Monthly goal, what's the **ONE THING** I can do **this week,** such that doing it everything else will be easier or unnecessary?

DAILY GOAL

Based on my Weekly goal, what's the **ONE THING** I can do **today,** such that doing it everything else will be easier or unnecessary?

RIGHT NOW

Based on my Daily goal, what's the **ONE THING** I can do **right now,** such that doing it everything else will be easier or unnecessary?

GOAL SETTING TO THE NOW

A MAP FOR THE BIG PICTURE AND A COMPASS FOR YOUR SMALLEST NEXT MOVE.

SOMEDAY GOAL

What's the **ONE THING** I want to do **someday**? What's the **ONE THING** I can do in my life that would **mean the most to me and the world**, such that by doing it everything else would be easier or unnecessary?

FIVE-YEAR GOAL

Based on my Someday goal, what's the **ONE THING** I can do **in the next five years,** such that doing it everything else will be easier or unnecessary?

ONE-YEAR GOAL

Based on my Five-year goal, what's the **ONE THING** I can do **this year,** such that doing it everything else will be easier or unnecessary?

MONTHLY GOAL

Based on my One-year goal, what's the **ONE THING** I can do **this month,** such that doing it everything else will be easier or unnecessary?

WEEKLY GOAL

Based on my Monthly goal, what's the **ONE THING** I can do **this week,** such that doing it everything else will be easier or unnecessary?

DAILY GOAL

Based on my Weekly goal, what's the **ONE THING** I can do **today,** such that doing it everything else will be easier or unnecessary?

RIGHT NOW

Based on my Daily goal, what's the **ONE THING** I can do **right now,** such that doing it everything else will be easier or unnecessary?

GOAL SETTING TO THE NOW

A MAP FOR THE BIG PICTURE AND A COMPASS FOR YOUR SMALLEST NEXT MOVE.

SOMEDAY GOAL

What's the **ONE THING** I want to do **someday**? What's the **ONE THING** I can do in my life that would **mean the most to me and the world**, such that by doing it everything else would be easier or unnecessary?

FIVE-YEAR GOAL

Based on my Someday goal, what's the **ONE THING** I can do **in the next five years,** such that doing it everything else will be easier or unnecessary?

ONE-YEAR GOAL

Based on my Five-year goal, what's the **ONE THING** I can do **this year,** such that doing it everything else will be easier or unnecessary?

MONTHLY GOAL

Based on my One-year goal, what's the **ONE THING** I can do **this month,** such that doing it everything else will be easier or unnecessary?

WEEKLY GOAL

Based on my Monthly goal, what's the **ONE THING** I can do **this week,** such that doing it everything else will be easier or unnecessary?

DAILY GOAL

Based on my Weekly goal, what's the **ONE THING** I can do **today,** such that doing it everything else will be easier or unnecessary?

RIGHT NOW

Based on my Daily goal, what's the **ONE THING** I can do **right now,** such that doing it everything else will be easier or unnecessary?

GOAL SETTING TO THE NOW

A MAP FOR THE BIG PICTURE AND A COMPASS FOR YOUR SMALLEST NEXT MOVE.

SOMEDAY GOAL

What's the **ONE THING** I want to do **someday**? What's the **ONE THING** I can do in my life that would **mean the most to me and the world**, such that by doing it everything else would be easier or unnecessary?

FIVE-YEAR GOAL

Based on my Someday goal, what's the **ONE THING** I can do in **the next five years,** such that doing it everything else will be easier or unnecessary?

ONE-YEAR GOAL

Based on my Five-year goal, what's the **ONE THING** I can do **this year,** such that doing it everything else will be easier or unnecessary?

MONTHLY GOAL

Based on my One-year goal, what's the **ONE THING** I can do **this month,** such that doing it everything else will be easier or unnecessary?

WEEKLY GOAL

Based on my Monthly goal, what's the **ONE THING** I can do **this week,** such that doing it everything else will be easier or unnecessary?

DAILY GOAL

Based on my Weekly goal, what's the **ONE THING** I can do **today,** such that doing it everything else will be easier or unnecessary?

RIGHT NOW

Based on my Daily goal, what's the **ONE THING** I can do **right now,** such that doing it everything else will be easier or unnecessary?

GOAL SETTING TO THE NOW

A MAP FOR THE BIG PICTURE AND A COMPASS FOR YOUR SMALLEST NEXT MOVE.

SOMEDAY GOAL

What's the **ONE THING** I want to do **someday**? What's the **ONE THING** I can do in my life that would **mean the most to me and the world**, such that by doing it everything else would be easier or unnecessary?

FIVE-YEAR GOAL

Based on my Someday goal, what's the **ONE THING** I can do in **the next five years,** such that doing it everything else will be easier or unnecessary?

ONE-YEAR GOAL

Based on my Five-year goal, what's the **ONE THING** I can do **this year,** such that doing it everything else will be easier or unnecessary?

MONTHLY GOAL

Based on my One-year goal, what's the **ONE THING** I can do **this month,** such that doing it everything else will be easier or unnecessary?

WEEKLY GOAL

Based on my Monthly goal, what's the **ONE THING** I can do **this week,** such that doing it everything else will be easier or unnecessary?

DAILY GOAL

Based on my Weekly goal, what's the **ONE THING** I can do **today,** such that doing it everything else will be easier or unnecessary?

RIGHT NOW

Based on my Daily goal, what's the **ONE THING** I can do **right now,** such that doing it everything else will be easier or unnecessary?

GOAL SETTING TO THE NOW

A MAP FOR THE BIG PICTURE AND A COMPASS FOR YOUR SMALLEST NEXT MOVE.

SOMEDAY GOAL

What's the **ONE THING** I want to do **someday**? What's the **ONE THING** I can do in my life that would **mean the most to me and the world**, such that by doing it everything else would be easier or unnecessary?

FIVE-YEAR GOAL

Based on my Someday goal, what's the **ONE THING** I can do **in the next five years,** such that doing it everything else will be easier or unnecessary?

ONE-YEAR GOAL

Based on my Five-year goal, what's the **ONE THING** I can do **this year,** such that doing it everything else will be easier or unnecessary?

MONTHLY GOAL

Based on my One-year goal, what's the **ONE THING** I can do **this month,** such that doing it everything else will be easier or unnecessary?

WEEKLY GOAL

Based on my Monthly goal, what's the **ONE THING** I can do **this week,** such that doing it everything else will be easier or unnecessary?

DAILY GOAL

Based on my Weekly goal, what's the **ONE THING** I can do **today,** such that doing it everything else will be easier or unnecessary?

RIGHT NOW

Based on my Daily goal, what's the **ONE THING** I can do **right now,** such that doing it everything else will be easier or unnecessary?

GOAL SETTING TO THE NOW

A MAP FOR THE BIG PICTURE AND A COMPASS FOR YOUR SMALLEST NEXT MOVE.

SOMEDAY GOAL

What's the **ONE THING** I want to do **someday**? What's the **ONE THING** I can do in my life that would **mean the most to me and the world**, such that by doing it everything else would be easier or unnecessary?

FIVE-YEAR GOAL

Based on my Someday goal, what's the **ONE THING** I can do in **the next five years,** such that doing it everything else will be easier or unnecessary?

ONE-YEAR GOAL

Based on my Five-year goal, what's the **ONE THING** I can do **this year,** such that doing it everything else will be easier or unnecessary?

MONTHLY GOAL

Based on my One-year goal, what's the **ONE THING** I can do **this month,** such that doing it everything else will be easier or unnecessary?

WEEKLY GOAL

Based on my Monthly goal, what's the **ONE THING** I can do **this week,** such that doing it everything else will be easier or unnecessary?

DAILY GOAL

Based on my Weekly goal, what's the **ONE THING** I can do **today,** such that doing it everything else will be easier or unnecessary?

RIGHT NOW

Based on my Daily goal, what's the **ONE THING** I can do **right now,** such that doing it everything else will be easier or unnecessary?

GOAL SETTING TO THE NOW

A MAP FOR THE BIG PICTURE AND A COMPASS FOR YOUR SMALLEST NEXT MOVE.

SOMEDAY GOAL

What's the **ONE THING** I want to do **someday**? What's the **ONE THING** I can do in my life that would **mean the most to me and the world**, such that by doing it everything else would be easier or unnecessary?

FIVE-YEAR GOAL

Based on my Someday goal, what's the **ONE THING** I can do in **the next five years,** such that doing it everything else will be easier or unnecessary?

ONE-YEAR GOAL

Based on my Five-year goal, what's the **ONE THING** I can do **this year,** such that doing it everything else will be easier or unnecessary?

MONTHLY GOAL

Based on my One-year goal, what's the **ONE THING** I can do **this month,** such that doing it everything else will be easier or unnecessary?

WEEKLY GOAL

Based on my Monthly goal, what's the **ONE THING** I can do **this week,** such that doing it everything else will be easier or unnecessary?

DAILY GOAL

Based on my Weekly goal, what's the **ONE THING** I can do **today,** such that doing it everything else will be easier or unnecessary?

RIGHT NOW

Based on my Daily goal, what's the **ONE THING** I can do **right now,** such that doing it everything else will be easier or unnecessary?

GOAL SETTING TO THE NOW

A MAP FOR THE BIG PICTURE AND A COMPASS FOR YOUR SMALLEST NEXT MOVE.

SOMEDAY GOAL

What's the **ONE THING** I want to do **someday**? What's the **ONE THING** I can do in my life that would **mean the most to me and the world**, such that by doing it everything else would be easier or unnecessary?

FIVE-YEAR GOAL

Based on my Someday goal, what's the **ONE THING** I can do in **the next five years,** such that doing it everything else will be easier or unnecessary?

ONE-YEAR GOAL

Based on my Five-year goal, what's the **ONE THING** I can do **this year,** such that doing it everything else will be easier or unnecessary?

MONTHLY GOAL

Based on my One-year goal, what's the **ONE THING** I can do **this month,** such that doing it everything else will be easier or unnecessary?

WEEKLY GOAL

Based on my Monthly goal, what's the **ONE THING** I can do **this week,** such that doing it everything else will be easier or unnecessary?

DAILY GOAL

Based on my Weekly goal, what's the **ONE THING** I can do **today,** such that doing it everything else will be easier or unnecessary?

RIGHT NOW

Based on my Daily goal, what's the **ONE THING** I can do **right now,** such that doing it everything else will be easier or unnecessary?

GOAL SETTING TO THE NOW

A MAP FOR THE BIG PICTURE AND A COMPASS FOR YOUR SMALLEST NEXT MOVE.

SOMEDAY GOAL

What's the **ONE THING** I want to do **someday**? What's the **ONE THING** I can do in my life that would **mean the most to me and the world**, such that by doing it everything else would be easier or unnecessary?

FIVE-YEAR GOAL

Based on my Someday goal, what's the **ONE THING** I can do **in the next five years,** such that doing it everything else will be easier or unnecessary?

ONE-YEAR GOAL

Based on my Five-year goal, what's the **ONE THING** I can do **this year,** such that doing it everything else will be easier or unnecessary?

MONTHLY GOAL

Based on my One-year goal, what's the **ONE THING** I can do **this month,** such that doing it everything else will be easier or unnecessary?

WEEKLY GOAL

Based on my Monthly goal, what's the **ONE THING** I can do **this week,** such that doing it everything else will be easier or unnecessary?

DAILY GOAL

Based on my Weekly goal, what's the **ONE THING** I can do **today,** such that doing it everything else will be easier or unnecessary?

RIGHT NOW

Based on my Daily goal, what's the **ONE THING** I can do **right now,** such that doing it everything else will be easier or unnecessary?

GOAL SETTING TO THE NOW

A MAP FOR THE BIG PICTURE AND A COMPASS FOR YOUR SMALLEST NEXT MOVE.

SOMEDAY GOAL

What's the **ONE THING** I want to do **someday**? What's the **ONE THING** I can do in my life that would **mean the most to me and the world**, such that by doing it everything else would be easier or unnecessary?

FIVE-YEAR GOAL

Based on my Someday goal, what's the **ONE THING** I can do in **the next five years,** such that doing it everything else will be easier or unnecessary?

ONE-YEAR GOAL

Based on my Five-year goal, what's the **ONE THING** I can do **this year,** such that doing it everything else will be easier or unnecessary?

MONTHLY GOAL

Based on my One-year goal, what's the **ONE THING** I can do **this month,** such that doing it everything else will be easier or unnecessary?

WEEKLY GOAL

Based on my Monthly goal, what's the **ONE THING** I can do **this week,** such that doing it everything else will be easier or unnecessary?

DAILY GOAL

Based on my Weekly goal, what's the **ONE THING** I can do **today,** such that doing it everything else will be easier or unnecessary?

RIGHT NOW

Based on my Daily goal, what's the **ONE THING** I can do **right now,** such that doing it everything else will be easier or unnecessary?

GOAL SETTING TO THE NOW

A MAP FOR THE BIG PICTURE AND A COMPASS FOR YOUR SMALLEST NEXT MOVE.

SOMEDAY GOAL

What's the **ONE THING** I want to do **someday**? What's the **ONE THING** I can do in my life that would **mean the most to me and the world**, such that by doing it everything else would be easier or unnecessary?

FIVE-YEAR GOAL

Based on my Someday goal, what's the **ONE THING** I can do in **the next five years,** such that doing it everything else will be easier or unnecessary?

ONE-YEAR GOAL

Based on my Five-year goal, what's the **ONE THING** I can do **this year,** such that doing it everything else will be easier or unnecessary?

MONTHLY GOAL

Based on my One-year goal, what's the **ONE THING** I can do **this month,** such that doing it everything else will be easier or unnecessary?

WEEKLY GOAL

Based on my Monthly goal, what's the **ONE THING** I can do **this week,** such that doing it everything else will be easier or unnecessary?

DAILY GOAL

Based on my Weekly goal, what's the **ONE THING** I can do **today,** such that doing it everything else will be easier or unnecessary?

RIGHT NOW

Based on my Daily goal, what's the **ONE THING** I can do **right now,** such that doing it everything else will be easier or unnecessary?

GOAL SETTING TO THE NOW

A MAP FOR THE BIG PICTURE AND A COMPASS FOR YOUR SMALLEST NEXT MOVE.

SOMEDAY GOAL

What's the **ONE THING** I want to do **someday**? What's the **ONE THING** I can do in my life that would **mean the most to me and the world**, such that by doing it everything else would be easier or unnecessary?

FIVE-YEAR GOAL

Based on my Someday goal, what's the **ONE THING** I can do in **the next five years,** such that doing it everything else will be easier or unnecessary?

ONE-YEAR GOAL

Based on my Five-year goal, what's the **ONE THING** I can do **this year,** such that doing it everything else will be easier or unnecessary?

MONTHLY GOAL

Based on my One-year goal, what's the **ONE THING** I can do **this month,** such that doing it everything else will be easier or unnecessary?

WEEKLY GOAL

Based on my Monthly goal, what's the **ONE THING** I can do **this week,** such that doing it everything else will be easier or unnecessary?

DAILY GOAL

Based on my Weekly goal, what's the **ONE THING** I can do **today,** such that doing it everything else will be easier or unnecessary?

RIGHT NOW

Based on my Daily goal, what's the **ONE THING** I can do **right now,** such that doing it everything else will be easier or unnecessary?

GOAL SETTING TO THE NOW

A MAP FOR THE BIG PICTURE AND A COMPASS FOR YOUR SMALLEST NEXT MOVE.

SOMEDAY GOAL

What's the **ONE THING** I want to do **someday**? What's the **ONE THING** I can do in my life that would **mean the most to me and the world**, such that by doing it everything else would be easier or unnecessary?

FIVE-YEAR GOAL

Based on my Someday goal, what's the **ONE THING** I can do in **the next five years,** such that doing it everything else will be easier or unnecessary?

ONE-YEAR GOAL

Based on my Five-year goal, what's the **ONE THING** I can do **this year,** such that doing it everything else will be easier or unnecessary?

MONTHLY GOAL

Based on my One-year goal, what's the **ONE THING** I can do **this month,** such that doing it everything else will be easier or unnecessary?

WEEKLY GOAL

Based on my Monthly goal, what's the **ONE THING** I can do **this week,** such that doing it everything else will be easier or unnecessary?

DAILY GOAL

Based on my Weekly goal, what's the **ONE THING** I can do **today,** such that doing it everything else will be easier or unnecessary?

RIGHT NOW

Based on my Daily goal, what's the **ONE THING** I can do **right now,** such that doing it everything else will be easier or unnecessary?

GOAL SETTING TO THE NOW

A MAP FOR THE BIG PICTURE AND A COMPASS FOR YOUR SMALLEST NEXT MOVE.

SOMEDAY GOAL

What's the **ONE THING** I want to do **someday**? What's the **ONE THING** I can do in my life that would **mean the most to me and the world**, such that by doing it everything else would be easier or unnecessary?

FIVE-YEAR GOAL

Based on my Someday goal, what's the **ONE THING** I can do in **the next five years,** such that doing it everything else will be easier or unnecessary?

ONE-YEAR GOAL

Based on my Five-year goal, what's the **ONE THING** I can do **this year,** such that doing it everything else will be easier or unnecessary?

MONTHLY GOAL

Based on my One-year goal, what's the **ONE THING** I can do **this month,** such that doing it everything else will be easier or unnecessary?

WEEKLY GOAL

Based on my Monthly goal, what's the **ONE THING** I can do **this week,** such that doing it everything else will be easier or unnecessary?

DAILY GOAL

Based on my Weekly goal, what's the **ONE THING** I can do **today,** such that doing it everything else will be easier or unnecessary?

RIGHT NOW

Based on my Daily goal, what's the **ONE THING** I can do **right now,** such that doing it everything else will be easier or unnecessary?

GOAL SETTING TO THE NOW

A MAP FOR THE BIG PICTURE AND A COMPASS FOR YOUR SMALLEST NEXT MOVE.

SOMEDAY GOAL

What's the **ONE THING** I want to do **someday**? What's the **ONE THING** I can do in my life that would **mean the most to me and the world**, such that by doing it everything else would be easier or unnecessary?

FIVE-YEAR GOAL

Based on my Someday goal, what's the **ONE THING** I can do in **the next five years,** such that doing it everything else will be easier or unnecessary?

ONE-YEAR GOAL

Based on my Five-year goal, what's the **ONE THING** I can do **this year,** such that doing it everything else will be easier or unnecessary?

MONTHLY GOAL

Based on my One-year goal, what's the **ONE THING** I can do **this month,** such that doing it everything else will be easier or unnecessary?

WEEKLY GOAL

Based on my Monthly goal, what's the **ONE THING** I can do **this week,** such that doing it everything else will be easier or unnecessary?

DAILY GOAL

Based on my Weekly goal, what's the **ONE THING** I can do **today,** such that doing it everything else will be easier or unnecessary?

RIGHT NOW

Based on my Daily goal, what's the **ONE THING** I can do **right now,** such that doing it everything else will be easier or unnecessary?

GOAL SETTING TO THE NOW

A MAP FOR THE BIG PICTURE AND A COMPASS FOR YOUR SMALLEST NEXT MOVE.

SOMEDAY GOAL

What's the **ONE THING** I want to do **someday**? What's the **ONE THING** I can do in my life that would **mean the most to me and the world**, such that by doing it everything else would be easier or unnecessary?

FIVE-YEAR GOAL

Based on my Someday goal, what's the **ONE THING** I can do in **the next five years,** such that doing it everything else will be easier or unnecessary?

ONE-YEAR GOAL

Based on my Five-year goal, what's the **ONE THING** I can do **this year,** such that doing it everything else will be easier or unnecessary?

MONTHLY GOAL

Based on my One-year goal, what's the **ONE THING** I can do **this month,** such that doing it everything else will be easier or unnecessary?

WEEKLY GOAL

Based on my Monthly goal, what's the **ONE THING** I can do **this week,** such that doing it everything else will be easier or unnecessary?

DAILY GOAL

Based on my Weekly goal, what's the **ONE THING** I can do **today,** such that doing it everything else will be easier or unnecessary?

RIGHT NOW

Based on my Daily goal, what's the **ONE THING** I can do **right now,** such that doing it everything else will be easier or unnecessary?

GOAL SETTING TO THE NOW

A MAP FOR THE BIG PICTURE AND A COMPASS FOR YOUR SMALLEST NEXT MOVE.

SOMEDAY GOAL

What's the **ONE THING** I want to do **someday**? What's the **ONE THING** I can do in my life that would **mean the most to me and the world**, such that by doing it everything else would be easier or unnecessary?

FIVE-YEAR GOAL

Based on my Someday goal, what's the **ONE THING** I can do **in the next five years,** such that doing it everything else will be easier or unnecessary?

ONE-YEAR GOAL

Based on my Five-year goal, what's the **ONE THING** I can do **this year,** such that doing it everything else will be easier or unnecessary?

MONTHLY GOAL

Based on my One-year goal, what's the **ONE THING** I can do **this month,** such that doing it everything else will be easier or unnecessary?

WEEKLY GOAL

Based on my Monthly goal, what's the **ONE THING** I can do **this week,** such that doing it everything else will be easier or unnecessary?

DAILY GOAL

Based on my Weekly goal, what's the **ONE THING** I can do **today,** such that doing it everything else will be easier or unnecessary?

RIGHT NOW

Based on my Daily goal, what's the **ONE THING** I can do **right now,** such that doing it everything else will be easier or unnecessary?

GOAL SETTING TO THE NOW

A MAP FOR THE BIG PICTURE AND A COMPASS FOR YOUR SMALLEST NEXT MOVE.

SOMEDAY GOAL

What's the **ONE THING** I want to do **someday**? What's the **ONE THING** I can do in my life that would **mean the most to me and the world**, such that by doing it everything else would be easier or unnecessary?

FIVE-YEAR GOAL

Based on my Someday goal, what's the **ONE THING** I can do in **the next five years,** such that doing it everything else will be easier or unnecessary?

ONE-YEAR GOAL

Based on my Five-year goal, what's the **ONE THING** I can do **this year,** such that doing it everything else will be easier or unnecessary?

MONTHLY GOAL

Based on my One-year goal, what's the **ONE THING** I can do **this month,** such that doing it everything else will be easier or unnecessary?

WEEKLY GOAL

Based on my Monthly goal, what's the **ONE THING** I can do **this week,** such that doing it everything else will be easier or unnecessary?

DAILY GOAL

Based on my Weekly goal, what's the **ONE THING** I can do **today,** such that doing it everything else will be easier or unnecessary?

RIGHT NOW

Based on my Daily goal, what's the **ONE THING** I can do **right now,** such that doing it everything else will be easier or unnecessary?

GOAL SETTING TO THE NOW

A MAP FOR THE BIG PICTURE AND A COMPASS FOR YOUR SMALLEST NEXT MOVE.

SOMEDAY GOAL

What's the **ONE THING** I want to do **someday**? What's the **ONE THING** I can do in my life that would **mean the most to me and the world**, such that by doing it everything else would be easier or unnecessary?

FIVE-YEAR GOAL

Based on my Someday goal, what's the **ONE THING** I can do in **the next five years,** such that doing it everything else will be easier or unnecessary?

ONE-YEAR GOAL

Based on my Five-year goal, what's the **ONE THING** I can do **this year,** such that doing it everything else will be easier or unnecessary?

MONTHLY GOAL

Based on my One-year goal, what's the **ONE THING** I can do **this month,** such that doing it everything else will be easier or unnecessary?

WEEKLY GOAL

Based on my Monthly goal, what's the **ONE THING** I can do **this week,** such that doing it everything else will be easier or unnecessary?

DAILY GOAL

Based on my Weekly goal, what's the **ONE THING** I can do **today,** such that doing it everything else will be easier or unnecessary?

RIGHT NOW

Based on my Daily goal, what's the **ONE THING** I can do **right now,** such that doing it everything else will be easier or unnecessary?

GOAL SETTING TO THE NOW

A MAP FOR THE BIG PICTURE AND A COMPASS FOR YOUR SMALLEST NEXT MOVE.

SOMEDAY GOAL

What's the **ONE THING** I want to do **someday**? What's the **ONE THING** I can do in my life that would **mean the most to me and the world**, such that by doing it everything else would be easier or unnecessary?

FIVE-YEAR GOAL

Based on my Someday goal, what's the **ONE THING** I can do in **the next five years,** such that doing it everything else will be easier or unnecessary?

ONE-YEAR GOAL

Based on my Five-year goal, what's the **ONE THING** I can do **this year,** such that doing it everything else will be easier or unnecessary?

MONTHLY GOAL

Based on my One-year goal, what's the **ONE THING** I can do **this month,** such that doing it everything else will be easier or unnecessary?

WEEKLY GOAL

Based on my Monthly goal, what's the **ONE THING** I can do **this week,** such that doing it everything else will be easier or unnecessary?

DAILY GOAL

Based on my Weekly goal, what's the **ONE THING** I can do **today,** such that doing it everything else will be easier or unnecessary?

RIGHT NOW

Based on my Daily goal, what's the **ONE THING** I can do **right now,** such that doing it everything else will be easier or unnecessary?

GOAL SETTING TO THE NOW

A MAP FOR THE BIG PICTURE AND A COMPASS FOR YOUR SMALLEST NEXT MOVE.

SOMEDAY GOAL

What's the **ONE THING** I want to do **someday**? What's the **ONE THING** I can do in my life that would **mean the most to me and the world**, such that by doing it everything else would be easier or unnecessary?

FIVE-YEAR GOAL

Based on my Someday goal, what's the **ONE THING** I can do in **the next five years,** such that doing it everything else will be easier or unnecessary?

ONE-YEAR GOAL

Based on my Five-year goal, what's the **ONE THING** I can do **this year,** such that doing it everything else will be easier or unnecessary?

MONTHLY GOAL

Based on my One-year goal, what's the **ONE THING** I can do **this month,** such that doing it everything else will be easier or unnecessary?

WEEKLY GOAL

Based on my Monthly goal, what's the **ONE THING** I can do **this week,** such that doing it everything else will be easier or unnecessary?

DAILY GOAL

Based on my Weekly goal, what's the **ONE THING** I can do **today,** such that doing it everything else will be easier or unnecessary?

RIGHT NOW

Based on my Daily goal, what's the **ONE THING** I can do **right now,** such that doing it everything else will be easier or unnecessary?

GOAL SETTING TO THE NOW

A MAP FOR THE BIG PICTURE AND A COMPASS FOR YOUR SMALLEST NEXT MOVE.

SOMEDAY GOAL

What's the **ONE THING** I want to do **someday**? What's the **ONE THING** I can do in my life that would **mean the most to me and the world**, such that by doing it everything else would be easier or unnecessary?

FIVE-YEAR GOAL

Based on my Someday goal, what's the **ONE THING** I can do in **the next five years,** such that doing it everything else will be easier or unnecessary?

ONE-YEAR GOAL

Based on my Five-year goal, what's the **ONE THING** I can do **this year,** such that doing it everything else will be easier or unnecessary?

MONTHLY GOAL

Based on my One-year goal, what's the **ONE THING** I can do **this month,** such that doing it everything else will be easier or unnecessary?

WEEKLY GOAL

Based on my Monthly goal, what's the **ONE THING** I can do **this week,** such that doing it everything else will be easier or unnecessary?

DAILY GOAL

Based on my Weekly goal, what's the **ONE THING** I can do **today,** such that doing it everything else will be easier or unnecessary?

RIGHT NOW

Based on my Daily goal, what's the **ONE THING** I can do **right now,** such that doing it everything else will be easier or unnecessary?

GOAL SETTING TO THE NOW

A MAP FOR THE BIG PICTURE AND A COMPASS FOR YOUR SMALLEST NEXT MOVE.

SOMEDAY GOAL

What's the **ONE THING** I want to do **someday**? What's the **ONE THING** I can do in my life that would **mean the most to me and the world**, such that by doing it everything else would be easier or unnecessary?

FIVE-YEAR GOAL

Based on my Someday goal, what's the **ONE THING** I can do in **the next five years,** such that doing it everything else will be easier or unnecessary?

ONE-YEAR GOAL

Based on my Five-year goal, what's the **ONE THING** I can do **this year,** such that doing it everything else will be easier or unnecessary?

MONTHLY GOAL

Based on my One-year goal, what's the **ONE THING** I can do **this month,** such that doing it everything else will be easier or unnecessary?

WEEKLY GOAL

Based on my Monthly goal, what's the **ONE THING** I can do **this week,** such that doing it everything else will be easier or unnecessary?

DAILY GOAL

Based on my Weekly goal, what's the **ONE THING** I can do **today,** such that doing it everything else will be easier or unnecessary?

RIGHT NOW

Based on my Daily goal, what's the **ONE THING** I can do **right now,** such that doing it everything else will be easier or unnecessary?

GOAL SETTING TO THE NOW

A MAP FOR THE BIG PICTURE AND A COMPASS FOR YOUR SMALLEST NEXT MOVE.

SOMEDAY GOAL

What's the **ONE THING** I want to do **someday**? What's the **ONE THING** I can do in my life that would **mean the most to me and the world**, such that by doing it everything else would be easier or unnecessary?

FIVE-YEAR GOAL

Based on my Someday goal, what's the **ONE THING** I can do in **the next five years**, such that doing it everything else will be easier or unnecessary?

ONE-YEAR GOAL

Based on my Five-year goal, what's the **ONE THING** I can do **this year**, such that doing it everything else will be easier or unnecessary?

MONTHLY GOAL

Based on my One-year goal, what's the **ONE THING** I can do **this month**, such that doing it everything else will be easier or unnecessary?

WEEKLY GOAL

Based on my Monthly goal, what's the **ONE THING** I can do **this week**, such that doing it everything else will be easier or unnecessary?

DAILY GOAL

Based on my Weekly goal, what's the **ONE THING** I can do **today**, such that doing it everything else will be easier or unnecessary?

RIGHT NOW

Based on my Daily goal, what's the **ONE THING** I can do **right now**, such that doing it everything else will be easier or unnecessary?

GOAL SETTING TO THE NOW

A MAP FOR THE BIG PICTURE AND A COMPASS FOR YOUR SMALLEST NEXT MOVE.

SOMEDAY GOAL

_____
_____
_____
_____

What's the **ONE THING** I want to do **someday**? What's the **ONE THING** I can do in my life that would **mean the most to me and the world**, such that by doing it everything else would be easier or unnecessary?

_____
_____

FIVE-YEAR GOAL

_____
_____
_____

Based on my Someday goal, what's the **ONE THING** I can do in **the next five years,** such that doing it everything else will be easier or unnecessary?

_____
_____

ONE-YEAR GOAL

_____
_____
_____

Based on my Five-year goal, what's the **ONE THING** I can do **this year,** such that doing it everything else will be easier or unnecessary?

_____
_____

MONTHLY GOAL

_____
_____
_____

Based on my One-year goal, what's the **ONE THING** I can do **this month,** such that doing it everything else will be easier or unnecessary?

_____
_____

WEEKLY GOAL

_____
_____
_____

Based on my Monthly goal, what's the **ONE THING** I can do **this week,** such that doing it everything else will be easier or unnecessary?

_____
_____

DAILY GOAL

_____
_____
_____

Based on my Weekly goal, what's the **ONE THING** I can do **today,** such that doing it everything else will be easier or unnecessary?

_____
_____

RIGHT NOW

Based on my Daily goal, what's the **ONE THING** I can do **right now,** such that doing it everything else will be easier or unnecessary?

_____
_____
_____
_____

GOAL SETTING TO THE NOW

A MAP FOR THE BIG PICTURE AND A COMPASS FOR YOUR SMALLEST NEXT MOVE.

SOMEDAY GOAL

What's the **ONE THING** I want to do **someday**? What's the **ONE THING** I can do in my life that would **mean the most to me and the world**, such that by doing it everything else would be easier or unnecessary?

FIVE-YEAR GOAL

Based on my Someday goal, what's the **ONE THING** I can do in **the next five years,** such that doing it everything else will be easier or unnecessary?

ONE-YEAR GOAL

Based on my Five-year goal, what's the **ONE THING** I can do **this year**, such that doing it everything else will be easier or unnecessary?

MONTHLY GOAL

Based on my One-year goal, what's the **ONE THING** I can do **this month,** such that doing it everything else will be easier or unnecessary?

WEEKLY GOAL

Based on my Monthly goal, what's the **ONE THING** I can do **this week**, such that doing it everything else will be easier or unnecessary?

DAILY GOAL

Based on my Weekly goal, what's the **ONE THING** I can do **today**, such that doing it everything else will be easier or unnecessary?

RIGHT NOW

Based on my Daily goal, what's the **ONE THING** I can do **right now,** such that doing it everything else will be easier or unnecessary?

GOAL SETTING TO THE NOW

A MAP FOR THE BIG PICTURE AND A COMPASS FOR YOUR SMALLEST NEXT MOVE.

SOMEDAY GOAL

What's the **ONE THING** I want to do **someday**? What's the **ONE THING** I can do in my life that would **mean the most to me and the world**, such that by doing it everything else would be easier or unnecessary?

FIVE-YEAR GOAL

Based on my Someday goal, what's the **ONE THING** I can do in **the next five years,** such that doing it everything else will be easier or unnecessary?

ONE-YEAR GOAL

Based on my Five-year goal, what's the **ONE THING** I can do **this year,** such that doing it everything else will be easier or unnecessary?

MONTHLY GOAL

Based on my One-year goal, what's the **ONE THING** I can do **this month,** such that doing it everything else will be easier or unnecessary?

WEEKLY GOAL

Based on my Monthly goal, what's the **ONE THING** I can do **this week,** such that doing it everything else will be easier or unnecessary?

DAILY GOAL

Based on my Weekly goal, what's the **ONE THING** I can do **today,** such that doing it everything else will be easier or unnecessary?

RIGHT NOW

Based on my Daily goal, what's the **ONE THING** I can do **right now,** such that doing it everything else will be easier or unnecessary?

GOAL SETTING TO THE NOW

A MAP FOR THE BIG PICTURE AND A COMPASS FOR YOUR SMALLEST NEXT MOVE.

SOMEDAY GOAL

What's the **ONE THING** I want to do **someday**? What's the **ONE THING** I can do in my life that would **mean the most to me and the world**, such that by doing it everything else would be easier or unnecessary?

FIVE-YEAR GOAL

Based on my Someday goal, what's the **ONE THING** I can do in **the next five years,** such that doing it everything else will be easier or unnecessary?

ONE-YEAR GOAL

Based on my Five-year goal, what's the **ONE THING** I can do **this year,** such that doing it everything else will be easier or unnecessary?

MONTHLY GOAL

Based on my One-year goal, what's the **ONE THING** I can do **this month,** such that doing it everything else will be easier or unnecessary?

WEEKLY GOAL

Based on my Monthly goal, what's the **ONE THING** I can do **this week,** such that doing it everything else will be easier or unnecessary?

DAILY GOAL

Based on my Weekly goal, what's the **ONE THING** I can do **today,** such that doing it everything else will be easier or unnecessary?

RIGHT NOW

Based on my Daily goal, what's the **ONE THING** I can do **right now,** such that doing it everything else will be easier or unnecessary?

GOAL SETTING TO THE NOW

A MAP FOR THE BIG PICTURE AND A COMPASS FOR YOUR SMALLEST NEXT MOVE.

SOMEDAY GOAL

What's the **ONE THING** I want to do **someday**? What's the **ONE THING** I can do in my life that would **mean the most to me and the world**, such that by doing it everything else would be easier or unnecessary?

FIVE-YEAR GOAL

Based on my Someday goal, what's the **ONE THING** I can do in **the next five years**, such that doing it everything else will be easier or unnecessary?

ONE-YEAR GOAL

Based on my Five-year goal, what's the **ONE THING** I can do **this year**, such that doing it everything else will be easier or unnecessary?

MONTHLY GOAL

Based on my One-year goal, what's the **ONE THING** I can do **this month**, such that doing it everything else will be easier or unnecessary?

WEEKLY GOAL

Based on my Monthly goal, what's the **ONE THING** I can do **this week**, such that doing it everything else will be easier or unnecessary?

DAILY GOAL

Based on my Weekly goal, what's the **ONE THING** I can do **today**, such that doing it everything else will be easier or unnecessary?

RIGHT NOW

Based on my Daily goal, what's the **ONE THING** I can do **right now**, such that doing it everything else will be easier or unnecessary?

GOAL SETTING TO THE NOW

A MAP FOR THE BIG PICTURE AND A COMPASS FOR YOUR SMALLEST NEXT MOVE.

SOMEDAY GOAL

What's the **ONE THING** I want to do **someday**? What's the **ONE THING** I can do in my life that would **mean the most to me and the world**, such that by doing it everything else would be easier or unnecessary?

FIVE-YEAR GOAL

Based on my Someday goal, what's the **ONE THING** I can do in **the next five years,** such that doing it everything else will be easier or unnecessary?

ONE-YEAR GOAL

Based on my Five-year goal, what's the **ONE THING** I can do **this year,** such that doing it everything else will be easier or unnecessary?

MONTHLY GOAL

Based on my One-year goal, what's the **ONE THING** I can do **this month,** such that doing it everything else will be easier or unnecessary?

WEEKLY GOAL

Based on my Monthly goal, what's the **ONE THING** I can do **this week,** such that doing it everything else will be easier or unnecessary?

DAILY GOAL

Based on my Weekly goal, what's the **ONE THING** I can do **today,** such that doing it everything else will be easier or unnecessary?

RIGHT NOW

Based on my Daily goal, what's the **ONE THING** I can do **right now,** such that doing it everything else will be easier or unnecessary?

GOAL SETTING TO THE NOW

A MAP FOR THE BIG PICTURE AND A COMPASS FOR YOUR SMALLEST NEXT MOVE.

SOMEDAY GOAL

What's the **ONE THING** I want to do **someday**? What's the **ONE THING** I can do in my life that would **mean the most to me and the world**, such that by doing it everything else would be easier or unnecessary?

FIVE-YEAR GOAL

Based on my Someday goal, what's the **ONE THING** I can do in **the next five years,** such that doing it everything else will be easier or unnecessary?

ONE-YEAR GOAL

Based on my Five-year goal, what's the **ONE THING** I can do **this year,** such that doing it everything else will be easier or unnecessary?

MONTHLY GOAL

Based on my One-year goal, what's the **ONE THING** I can do **this month,** such that doing it everything else will be easier or unnecessary?

WEEKLY GOAL

Based on my Monthly goal, what's the **ONE THING** I can do **this week,** such that doing it everything else will be easier or unnecessary?

DAILY GOAL

Based on my Weekly goal, what's the **ONE THING** I can do **today,** such that doing it everything else will be easier or unnecessary?

RIGHT NOW

Based on my Daily goal, what's the **ONE THING** I can do **right now,** such that doing it everything else will be easier or unnecessary?

GOAL SETTING TO THE NOW

A MAP FOR THE BIG PICTURE AND A COMPASS FOR YOUR SMALLEST NEXT MOVE.

SOMEDAY GOAL

What's the **ONE THING** I want to do **someday**? What's the **ONE THING** I can do in my life that would **mean the most to me and the world**, such that by doing it everything else would be easier or unnecessary?

FIVE-YEAR GOAL

Based on my Someday goal, what's the **ONE THING** I can do in **the next five years,** such that doing it everything else will be easier or unnecessary?

ONE-YEAR GOAL

Based on my Five-year goal, what's the **ONE THING** I can do **this year,** such that doing it everything else will be easier or unnecessary?

MONTHLY GOAL

Based on my One-year goal, what's the **ONE THING** I can do **this month,** such that doing it everything else will be easier or unnecessary?

WEEKLY GOAL

Based on my Monthly goal, what's the **ONE THING** I can do **this week,** such that doing it everything else will be easier or unnecessary?

DAILY GOAL

Based on my Weekly goal, what's the **ONE THING** I can do **today,** such that doing it everything else will be easier or unnecessary?

RIGHT NOW

Based on my Daily goal, what's the **ONE THING** I can do **right now,** such that doing it everything else will be easier or unnecessary?

GOAL SETTING TO THE NOW

A MAP FOR THE BIG PICTURE AND A COMPASS FOR YOUR SMALLEST NEXT MOVE.

SOMEDAY GOAL

What's the **ONE THING** I want to do **someday**? What's the **ONE THING** I can do in my life that would **mean the most to me and the world**, such that by doing it everything else would be easier or unnecessary?

FIVE-YEAR GOAL

Based on my Someday goal, what's the **ONE THING** I can do in **the next five years,** such that doing it everything else will be easier or unnecessary?

ONE-YEAR GOAL

Based on my Five-year goal, what's the **ONE THING** I can do **this year,** such that doing it everything else will be easier or unnecessary?

MONTHLY GOAL

Based on my One-year goal, what's the **ONE THING** I can do **this month,** such that doing it everything else will be easier or unnecessary?

WEEKLY GOAL

Based on my Monthly goal, what's the **ONE THING** I can do **this week,** such that doing it everything else will be easier or unnecessary?

DAILY GOAL

Based on my Weekly goal, what's the **ONE THING** I can do **today,** such that doing it everything else will be easier or unnecessary?

RIGHT NOW

Based on my Daily goal, what's the **ONE THING** I can do **right now,** such that doing it everything else will be easier or unnecessary?

GOAL SETTING TO THE NOW

A MAP FOR THE BIG PICTURE AND A COMPASS FOR YOUR SMALLEST NEXT MOVE.

SOMEDAY GOAL

What's the **ONE THING** I want to do **someday**? What's the **ONE THING** I can do in my life that would **mean the most to me and the world**, such that by doing it everything else would be easier or unnecessary?

FIVE-YEAR GOAL

Based on my Someday goal, what's the **ONE THING** I can do in **the next five years,** such that doing it everything else will be easier or unnecessary?

ONE-YEAR GOAL

Based on my Five-year goal, what's the **ONE THING** I can do **this year**, such that doing it everything else will be easier or unnecessary?

MONTHLY GOAL

Based on my One-year goal, what's the **ONE THING** I can do **this month,** such that doing it everything else will be easier or unnecessary?

WEEKLY GOAL

Based on my Monthly goal, what's the **ONE THING** I can do **this week**, such that doing it everything else will be easier or unnecessary?

DAILY GOAL

Based on my Weekly goal, what's the **ONE THING** I can do **today,** such that doing it everything else will be easier or unnecessary?

RIGHT NOW

Based on my Daily goal, what's the **ONE THING** I can do **right now,** such that doing it everything else will be easier or unnecessary?

GOAL SETTING TO THE NOW

A MAP FOR THE BIG PICTURE AND A COMPASS FOR YOUR SMALLEST NEXT MOVE.

SOMEDAY GOAL

What's the **ONE THING** I want to do **someday**? What's the **ONE THING** I can do in my life that would **mean the most to me and the world**, such that by doing it everything else would be easier or unnecessary?

FIVE-YEAR GOAL

Based on my Someday goal, what's the **ONE THING** I can do in **the next five years,** such that doing it everything else will be easier or unnecessary?

ONE-YEAR GOAL

Based on my Five-year goal, what's the **ONE THING** I can do **this year,** such that doing it everything else will be easier or unnecessary?

MONTHLY GOAL

Based on my One-year goal, what's the **ONE THING** I can do **this month,** such that doing it everything else will be easier or unnecessary?

WEEKLY GOAL

Based on my Monthly goal, what's the **ONE THING** I can do **this week,** such that doing it everything else will be easier or unnecessary?

DAILY GOAL

Based on my Weekly goal, what's the **ONE THING** I can do **today,** such that doing it everything else will be easier or unnecessary?

RIGHT NOW

Based on my Daily goal, what's the **ONE THING** I can do **right now,** such that doing it everything else will be easier or unnecessary?

GOAL SETTING TO THE NOW

A MAP FOR THE BIG PICTURE AND A COMPASS FOR YOUR SMALLEST NEXT MOVE.

SOMEDAY GOAL

What's the **ONE THING** I want to do **someday**? What's the **ONE THING** I can do in my life that would **mean the most to me and the world**, such that by doing it everything else would be easier or unnecessary?

FIVE-YEAR GOAL

Based on my Someday goal, what's the **ONE THING** I can do in **the next five years,** such that doing it everything else will be easier or unnecessary?

ONE-YEAR GOAL

Based on my Five-year goal, what's the **ONE THING** I can do **this year**, such that doing it everything else will be easier or unnecessary?

MONTHLY GOAL

Based on my One-year goal, what's the **ONE THING** I can do **this month,** such that doing it everything else will be easier or unnecessary?

WEEKLY GOAL

Based on my Monthly goal, what's the **ONE THING** I can do **this week**, such that doing it everything else will be easier or unnecessary?

DAILY GOAL

Based on my Weekly goal, what's the **ONE THING** I can do **today**, such that doing it everything else will be easier or unnecessary?

RIGHT NOW

Based on my Daily goal, what's the **ONE THING** I can do **right now**, such that doing it everything else will be easier or unnecessary?

GOAL SETTING TO THE NOW

A MAP FOR THE BIG PICTURE AND A COMPASS FOR YOUR SMALLEST NEXT MOVE.

SOMEDAY GOAL

What's the **ONE THING** I want to do **someday**? What's the **ONE THING** I can do in my life that would **mean the most to me and the world**, such that by doing it everything else would be easier or unnecessary?

FIVE-YEAR GOAL

Based on my Someday goal, what's the **ONE THING** I can do in **the next five years,** such that doing it everything else will be easier or unnecessary?

ONE-YEAR GOAL

Based on my Five-year goal, what's the **ONE THING** I can do **this year,** such that doing it everything else will be easier or unnecessary?

MONTHLY GOAL

Based on my One-year goal, what's the **ONE THING** I can do **this month,** such that doing it everything else will be easier or unnecessary?

WEEKLY GOAL

Based on my Monthly goal, what's the **ONE THING** I can do **this week,** such that doing it everything else will be easier or unnecessary?

DAILY GOAL

Based on my Weekly goal, what's the **ONE THING** I can do **today,** such that doing it everything else will be easier or unnecessary?

RIGHT NOW

Based on my Daily goal, what's the **ONE THING** I can do **right now,** such that doing it everything else will be easier or unnecessary?

GOAL SETTING TO THE NOW

A MAP FOR THE BIG PICTURE AND A COMPASS FOR YOUR SMALLEST NEXT MOVE.

SOMEDAY GOAL

What's the **ONE THING** I want to do **someday**? What's the **ONE THING** I can do in my life that would **mean the most to me and the world**, such that by doing it everything else would be easier or unnecessary?

FIVE-YEAR GOAL

Based on my Someday goal, what's the **ONE THING** I can do in **the next five years,** such that doing it everything else will be easier or unnecessary?

ONE-YEAR GOAL

Based on my Five-year goal, what's the **ONE THING** I can do **this year,** such that doing it everything else will be easier or unnecessary?

MONTHLY GOAL

Based on my One-year goal, what's the **ONE THING** I can do **this month,** such that doing it everything else will be easier or unnecessary?

WEEKLY GOAL

Based on my Monthly goal, what's the **ONE THING** I can do **this week,** such that doing it everything else will be easier or unnecessary?

DAILY GOAL

Based on my Weekly goal, what's the **ONE THING** I can do **today,** such that doing it everything else will be easier or unnecessary?

RIGHT NOW

Based on my Daily goal, what's the **ONE THING** I can do **right now,** such that doing it everything else will be easier or unnecessary?

GOAL SETTING TO THE NOW

A MAP FOR THE BIG PICTURE AND A COMPASS FOR YOUR SMALLEST NEXT MOVE.

SOMEDAY GOAL

What's the **ONE THING** I want to do **someday**? What's the **ONE THING** I can do in my life that would **mean the most to me and the world**, such that by doing it everything else would be easier or unnecessary?

FIVE-YEAR GOAL

Based on my Someday goal, what's the **ONE THING** I can do in **the next five years,** such that doing it everything else will be easier or unnecessary?

ONE-YEAR GOAL

Based on my Five-year goal, what's the **ONE THING** I can do **this year,** such that doing it everything else will be easier or unnecessary?

MONTHLY GOAL

Based on my One-year goal, what's the **ONE THING** I can do **this month,** such that doing it everything else will be easier or unnecessary?

WEEKLY GOAL

Based on my Monthly goal, what's the **ONE THING** I can do **this week,** such that doing it everything else will be easier or unnecessary?

DAILY GOAL

Based on my Weekly goal, what's the **ONE THING** I can do **today,** such that doing it everything else will be easier or unnecessary?

RIGHT NOW

Based on my Daily goal, what's the **ONE THING** I can do **right now,** such that doing it everything else will be easier or unnecessary?

GOAL SETTING TO THE NOW

A MAP FOR THE BIG PICTURE AND A COMPASS FOR YOUR SMALLEST NEXT MOVE.

SOMEDAY GOAL

What's the **ONE THING** I want to do **someday**? What's the **ONE THING** I can do in my life that would **mean the most to me and the world**, such that by doing it everything else would be easier or unnecessary?

FIVE-YEAR GOAL

Based on my Someday goal, what's the **ONE THING** I can do in **the next five years,** such that doing it everything else will be easier or unnecessary?

ONE-YEAR GOAL

Based on my Five-year goal, what's the **ONE THING** I can do **this year,** such that doing it everything else will be easier or unnecessary?

MONTHLY GOAL

Based on my One-year goal, what's the **ONE THING** I can do **this month,** such that doing it everything else will be easier or unnecessary?

WEEKLY GOAL

Based on my Monthly goal, what's the **ONE THING** I can do **this week,** such that doing it everything else will be easier or unnecessary?

DAILY GOAL

Based on my Weekly goal, what's the **ONE THING** I can do **today,** such that doing it everything else will be easier or unnecessary?

RIGHT NOW

Based on my Daily goal, what's the **ONE THING** I can do **right now,** such that doing it everything else will be easier or unnecessary?

GOAL SETTING TO THE NOW

A MAP FOR THE BIG PICTURE AND A COMPASS FOR YOUR SMALLEST NEXT MOVE.

SOMEDAY GOAL

What's the **ONE THING** I want to do **someday**? What's the **ONE THING** I can do in my life that would **mean the most to me and the world**, such that by doing it everything else would be easier or unnecessary?

FIVE-YEAR GOAL

Based on my Someday goal, what's the **ONE THING** I can do in **the next five years,** such that doing it everything else will be easier or unnecessary?

ONE-YEAR GOAL

Based on my Five-year goal, what's the **ONE THING** I can do **this year,** such that doing it everything else will be easier or unnecessary?

MONTHLY GOAL

Based on my One-year goal, what's the **ONE THING** I can do **this month,** such that doing it everything else will be easier or unnecessary?

WEEKLY GOAL

Based on my Monthly goal, what's the **ONE THING** I can do **this week,** such that doing it everything else will be easier or unnecessary?

DAILY GOAL

Based on my Weekly goal, what's the **ONE THING** I can do **today,** such that doing it everything else will be easier or unnecessary?

RIGHT NOW

Based on my Daily goal, what's the **ONE THING** I can do **right now,** such that doing it everything else will be easier or unnecessary?

GOAL SETTING TO THE NOW

A MAP FOR THE BIG PICTURE AND A COMPASS FOR YOUR SMALLEST NEXT MOVE.

SOMEDAY GOAL

What's the **ONE THING** I want to do **someday**? What's the **ONE THING** I can do in my life that would **mean the most to me and the world**, such that by doing it everything else would be easier or unnecessary?

FIVE-YEAR GOAL

Based on my Someday goal, what's the **ONE THING** I can do in **the next five years**, such that doing it everything else will be easier or unnecessary?

ONE-YEAR GOAL

Based on my Five-year goal, what's the **ONE THING** I can do **this year**, such that doing it everything else will be easier or unnecessary?

MONTHLY GOAL

Based on my One-year goal, what's the **ONE THING** I can do **this month**, such that doing it everything else will be easier or unnecessary?

WEEKLY GOAL

Based on my Monthly goal, what's the **ONE THING** I can do **this week**, such that doing it everything else will be easier or unnecessary?

DAILY GOAL

Based on my Weekly goal, what's the **ONE THING** I can do **today**, such that doing it everything else will be easier or unnecessary?

RIGHT NOW

Based on my Daily goal, what's the **ONE THING** I can do **right now**, such that doing it everything else will be easier or unnecessary?

IMPROVEMENT SHEET

PHYSICAL HEALTH

MENTAL HEALTH

PERSONAL LIFE

KEY RELATIONSHIPS

CAREER

FINANCES

FIND THE LEAD DOMINO IN ALL AREAS OF YOUR LIFE, AND WHACK AWAY AT IT UNTIL IT FALLS.

IMPROVEMENT SHEET

FIND THE LEAD DOMINO IN ALL AREAS OF YOUR LIFE,
AND WHACK AWAY AT IT UNTIL IT FALLS.

PHYSICAL HEALTH

How can I improve my physical health?

For my **physical health**, what's the **ONE THING** I can do, such that doing it everything else will be easier or unnecessary?

MENTAL HEALTH

How can I improve my mental health?

For my **mental health**, what's the **ONE THING** I can do, such that doing it everything else will be easier or unnecessary?

PERSONAL LIFE

How can I improve my personal life?

For my **personal life**, what's the **ONE THING** I can do, such that doing it everything else will be easier or unnecessary?

KEY RELATIONSHIPS

How can I improve my key relationships?

For my **key relationships**, what's the **ONE THING** I can do, such that doing it everything else will be easier or unnecessary?

CAREER

How can I improve my career?

For my **career**, what's the **ONE THING** I can do, such that doing it everything else will be easier or unnecessary?

FINANCES

How can I improve my finances?

For my **finances**, what's the **ONE THING** I can do, such that doing it everything else will be easier or unnecessary?

IMPROVEMENT SHEET

FIND THE LEAD DOMINO IN ALL AREAS OF YOUR LIFE,
AND WHACK AWAY AT IT UNTIL IT FALLS.

PHYSICAL HEALTH

How can I improve my physical health?

For my **physical health**, what's the **ONE THING** I can do, such that doing it everything else will be easier or unnecessary?

MENTAL HEALTH

How can I improve my mental health?

For my **mental health**, what's the **ONE THING** I can do, such that doing it everything else will be easier or unnecessary?

PERSONAL LIFE

How can I improve my personal life?

For my **personal life**, what's the **ONE THING** I can do, such that doing it everything else will be easier or unnecessary?

KEY RELATIONSHIPS

How can I improve my key relationships?

For my **key relationships**, what's the **ONE THING** I can do, such that doing it everything else will be easier or unnecessary?

CAREER

How can I improve my career?

For my **career**, what's the **ONE THING** I can do, such that doing it everything else will be easier or unnecessary?

FINANCES

How can I improve my finances?

For my **finances**, what's the **ONE THING** I can do, such that doing it everything else will be easier or unnecessary?

IMPROVEMENT SHEET

FIND THE LEAD DOMINO IN ALL AREAS OF YOUR LIFE,
AND WHACK AWAY AT IT UNTIL IT FALLS.

PHYSICAL HEALTH

How can I improve my physical health?

For my **physical health**, what's the **ONE THING** I can do, such that doing it everything else will be easier or unnecessary?

MENTAL HEALTH

How can I improve my mental health?

For my **mental health**, what's the **ONE THING** I can do, such that doing it everything else will be easier or unnecessary?

PERSONAL LIFE

How can I improve my personal life?

For my **personal life**, what's the **ONE THING** I can do, such that doing it everything else will be easier or unnecessary?

KEY RELATIONSHIPS

How can I improve my key relationships?

For my **key relationships**, what's the **ONE THING** I can do, such that doing it everything else will be easier or unnecessary?

CAREER

How can I improve my career?

For my **career**, what's the **ONE THING** I can do, such that doing it everything else will be easier or unnecessary?

FINANCES

How can I improve my finances?

For my **finances**, what's the **ONE THING** I can do, such that doing it everything else will be easier or unnecessary?

IMPROVEMENT SHEET

FIND THE LEAD DOMINO IN ALL AREAS OF YOUR LIFE,
AND WHACK AWAY AT IT UNTIL IT FALLS.

PHYSICAL HEALTH

How can I improve my physical health?

For my **physical health**, what's the **ONE THING** I can do, such that doing it everything else will be easier or unnecessary?

MENTAL HEALTH

How can I improve my mental health?

For my **mental health**, what's the **ONE THING** I can do, such that doing it everything else will be easier or unnecessary?

PERSONAL LIFE

How can I improve my personal life?

For my **personal life**, what's the **ONE THING** I can do, such that doing it everything else will be easier or unnecessary?

KEY RELATIONSHIPS

How can I improve my key relationships?

For my **key relationships**, what's the **ONE THING** I can do, such that doing it everything else will be easier or unnecessary?

CAREER

How can I improve my career?

For my **career**, what's the **ONE THING** I can do, such that doing it everything else will be easier or unnecessary?

FINANCES

How can I improve my finances?

For my **finances**, what's the **ONE THING** I can do, such that doing it everything else will be easier or unnecessary?

IMPROVEMENT SHEET

FIND THE LEAD DOMINO IN ALL AREAS OF YOUR LIFE,
AND WHACK AWAY AT IT UNTIL IT FALLS.

PHYSICAL HEALTH

How can I improve my physical health?

For my **physical health**, what's the **ONE THING** I can do, such that doing it everything else will be easier or unnecessary?

MENTAL HEALTH

How can I improve my mental health?

For my **mental health**, what's the **ONE THING** I can do, such that doing it everything else will be easier or unnecessary?

PERSONAL LIFE

How can I improve my personal life?

For my **personal life**, what's the **ONE THING** I can do, such that doing it everything else will be easier or unnecessary?

KEY RELATIONSHIPS

How can I improve my key relationships?

For my **key relationships**, what's the **ONE THING** I can do, such that doing it everything else will be easier or unnecessary?

CAREER

How can I improve my career?

For my **career**, what's the **ONE THING** I can do, such that doing it everything else will be easier or unnecessary?

FINANCES

How can I improve my finances?

For my **finances**, what's the **ONE THING** I can do, such that doing it everything else will be easier or unnecessary?

IMPROVEMENT SHEET

FIND THE LEAD DOMINO IN ALL AREAS OF YOUR LIFE,
AND WHACK AWAY AT IT UNTIL IT FALLS.

PHYSICAL HEALTH

How can I improve my physical health?

For my **physical health**, what's the **ONE THING** I can do, such that doing it everything else will be easier or unnecessary?

MENTAL HEALTH

How can I improve my mental health?

For my **mental health**, what's the **ONE THING** I can do, such that doing it everything else will be easier or unnecessary?

PERSONAL LIFE

How can I improve my personal life?

For my **personal life**, what's the **ONE THING** I can do, such that doing it everything else will be easier or unnecessary?

KEY RELATIONSHIPS

How can I improve my key relationships?

For my **key relationships**, what's the **ONE THING** I can do, such that doing it everything else will be easier or unnecessary?

CAREER

How can I improve my career?

For my **career**, what's the **ONE THING** I can do, such that doing it everything else will be easier or unnecessary?

FINANCES

How can I improve my finances?

For my **finances**, what's the **ONE THING** I can do, such that doing it everything else will be easier or unnecessary?

IMPROVEMENT SHEET

FIND THE LEAD DOMINO IN ALL AREAS OF YOUR LIFE,
AND WHACK AWAY AT IT UNTIL IT FALLS.

PHYSICAL HEALTH

How can I improve my physical health?

For my **physical health**, what's the **ONE THING** I can do, such that doing it everything else will be easier or unnecessary?

MENTAL HEALTH

How can I improve my mental health?

For my **mental health**, what's the **ONE THING** I can do, such that doing it everything else will be easier or unnecessary?

PERSONAL LIFE

How can I improve my personal life?

For my **personal life**, what's the **ONE THING** I can do, such that doing it everything else will be easier or unnecessary?

KEY RELATIONSHIPS

How can I improve my key relationships?

For my **key relationships**, what's the **ONE THING** I can do, such that doing it everything else will be easier or unnecessary?

CAREER

How can I improve my career?

For my **career**, what's the **ONE THING** I can do, such that doing it everything else will be easier or unnecessary?

FINANCES

How can I improve my finances?

For my **finances**, what's the **ONE THING** I can do, such that doing it everything else will be easier or unnecessary?

IMPROVEMENT SHEET

FIND THE LEAD DOMINO IN ALL AREAS OF YOUR LIFE,
AND WHACK AWAY AT IT UNTIL IT FALLS.

PHYSICAL HEALTH

How can I improve my physical health?

For my **physical health**, what's the **ONE THING** I can do, such that doing it everything else will be easier or unnecessary?

MENTAL HEALTH

How can I improve my mental health?

For my **mental health**, what's the **ONE THING** I can do, such that doing it everything else will be easier or unnecessary?

PERSONAL LIFE

How can I improve my personal life?

For my **personal life**, what's the **ONE THING** I can do, such that doing it everything else will be easier or unnecessary?

KEY RELATIONSHIPS

How can I improve my key relationships?

For my **key relationships**, what's the **ONE THING** I can do, such that doing it everything else will be easier or unnecessary?

CAREER

How can I improve my career?

For my **career**, what's the **ONE THING** I can do, such that doing it everything else will be easier or unnecessary?

FINANCES

How can I improve my finances?

For my **finances**, what's the **ONE THING** I can do, such that doing it everything else will be easier or unnecessary?

IMPROVEMENT SHEET

FIND THE LEAD DOMINO IN ALL AREAS OF YOUR LIFE,
AND WHACK AWAY AT IT UNTIL IT FALLS.

PHYSICAL HEALTH

How can I improve my physical health?

For my **physical health**, what's the **ONE THING** I can do, such that doing it everything else will be easier or unnecessary?

MENTAL HEALTH

How can I improve my mental health?

For my **mental health**, what's the **ONE THING** I can do, such that doing it everything else will be easier or unnecessary?

PERSONAL LIFE

How can I improve my personal life?

For my **personal life**, what's the **ONE THING** I can do, such that doing it everything else will be easier or unnecessary?

KEY RELATIONSHIPS

How can I improve my key relationships?

For my **key relationships**, what's the **ONE THING** I can do, such that doing it everything else will be easier or unnecessary?

CAREER

How can I improve my career?

For my **career**, what's the **ONE THING** I can do, such that doing it everything else will be easier or unnecessary?

FINANCES

How can I improve my finances?

For my **finances**, what's the **ONE THING** I can do, such that doing it everything else will be easier or unnecessary?

IMPROVEMENT SHEET

FIND THE LEAD DOMINO IN ALL AREAS OF YOUR LIFE,
AND WHACK AWAY AT IT UNTIL IT FALLS.

PHYSICAL HEALTH

How can I improve my physical health?

For my **physical health**, what's the **ONE THING** I can do, such that doing it everything else will be easier or unnecessary?

MENTAL HEALTH

How can I improve my mental health?

For my **mental health**, what's the **ONE THING** I can do, such that doing it everything else will be easier or unnecessary?

PERSONAL LIFE

How can I improve my personal life?

For my **personal life**, what's the **ONE THING** I can do, such that doing it everything else will be easier or unnecessary?

KEY RELATIONSHIPS

How can I improve my key relationships?

For my **key relationships**, what's the **ONE THING** I can do, such that doing it everything else will be easier or unnecessary?

CAREER

How can I improve my career?

For my **career**, what's the **ONE THING** I can do, such that doing it everything else will be easier or unnecessary?

FINANCES

How can I improve my finances?

For my **finances**, what's the **ONE THING** I can do, such that doing it everything else will be easier or unnecessary?

IMPROVEMENT SHEET

FIND THE LEAD DOMINO IN ALL AREAS OF YOUR LIFE,
AND WHACK AWAY AT IT UNTIL IT FALLS.

PHYSICAL HEALTH

How can I improve my physical health?

For my **physical health**, what's the **ONE THING** I can do, such that doing it everything else will be easier or unnecessary?

MENTAL HEALTH

How can I improve my mental health?

For my **mental health**, what's the **ONE THING** I can do, such that doing it everything else will be easier or unnecessary?

PERSONAL LIFE

How can I improve my personal life?

For my **personal life**, what's the **ONE THING** I can do, such that doing it everything else will be easier or unnecessary?

KEY RELATIONSHIPS

How can I improve my key relationships?

For my **key relationships**, what's the **ONE THING** I can do, such that doing it everything else will be easier or unnecessary?

CAREER

How can I improve my career?

For my **career**, what's the **ONE THING** I can do, such that doing it everything else will be easier or unnecessary?

FINANCES

How can I improve my finances?

For my **finances**, what's the **ONE THING** I can do, such that doing it everything else will be easier or unnecessary?

IMPROVEMENT SHEET

FIND THE LEAD DOMINO IN ALL AREAS OF YOUR LIFE,
AND WHACK AWAY AT IT UNTIL IT FALLS.

PHYSICAL HEALTH

How can I improve my physical health?

For my **physical health**, what's the **ONE THING** I can do, such that doing it everything else will be easier or unnecessary?

MENTAL HEALTH

How can I improve my mental health?

For my **mental health**, what's the **ONE THING** I can do, such that doing it everything else will be easier or unnecessary?

PERSONAL LIFE

How can I improve my personal life?

For my **personal life**, what's the **ONE THING** I can do, such that doing it everything else will be easier or unnecessary?

KEY RELATIONSHIPS

How can I improve my key relationships?

For my **key relationships**, what's the **ONE THING** I can do, such that doing it everything else will be easier or unnecessary?

CAREER

How can I improve my career?

For my **career**, what's the **ONE THING** I can do, such that doing it everything else will be easier or unnecessary?

FINANCES

How can I improve my finances?

For my **finances**, what's the **ONE THING** I can do, such that doing it everything else will be easier or unnecessary?

IMPROVEMENT SHEET

FIND THE LEAD DOMINO IN ALL AREAS OF YOUR LIFE,
AND WHACK AWAY AT IT UNTIL IT FALLS.

PHYSICAL HEALTH

How can I improve my physical health?

For my **physical health**, what's the **ONE THING** I can do, such that doing it everything else will be easier or unnecessary?

MENTAL HEALTH

How can I improve my mental health?

For my **mental health**, what's the **ONE THING** I can do, such that doing it everything else will be easier or unnecessary?

PERSONAL LIFE

How can I improve my personal life?

For my **personal life**, what's the **ONE THING** I can do, such that doing it everything else will be easier or unnecessary?

KEY RELATIONSHIPS

How can I improve my key relationships?

For my **key relationships**, what's the **ONE THING** I can do, such that doing it everything else will be easier or unnecessary?

CAREER

How can I improve my career?

For my **career**, what's the **ONE THING** I can do, such that doing it everything else will be easier or unnecessary?

FINANCES

How can I improve my finances?

For my **finances**, what's the **ONE THING** I can do, such that doing it everything else will be easier or unnecessary?

IMPROVEMENT SHEET

FIND THE LEAD DOMINO IN ALL AREAS OF YOUR LIFE,
AND WHACK AWAY AT IT UNTIL IT FALLS.

PHYSICAL HEALTH

How can I improve my physical health?

For my **physical health**, what's the **ONE THING** I can do, such that doing it everything else will be easier or unnecessary?

MENTAL HEALTH

How can I improve my mental health?

For my **mental health**, what's the **ONE THING** I can do, such that doing it everything else will be easier or unnecessary?

PERSONAL LIFE

How can I improve my personal life?

For my **personal life**, what's the **ONE THING** I can do, such that doing it everything else will be easier or unnecessary?

KEY RELATIONSHIPS

How can I improve my key relationships?

For my **key relationships**, what's the **ONE THING** I can do, such that doing it everything else will be easier or unnecessary?

CAREER

How can I improve my career?

For my **career**, what's the **ONE THING** I can do, such that doing it everything else will be easier or unnecessary?

FINANCES

How can I improve my finances?

For my **finances**, what's the **ONE THING** I can do, such that doing it everything else will be easier or unnecessary?

IMPROVEMENT SHEET

FIND THE LEAD DOMINO IN ALL AREAS OF YOUR LIFE,
AND WHACK AWAY AT IT UNTIL IT FALLS.

PHYSICAL HEALTH

How can I improve my physical health?

For my **physical health**, what's the **ONE THING** I can do, such that doing it everything else will be easier or unnecessary?

MENTAL HEALTH

How can I improve my mental health?

For my **mental health**, what's the **ONE THING** I can do, such that doing it everything else will be easier or unnecessary?

PERSONAL LIFE

How can I improve my personal life?

For my **personal life**, what's the **ONE THING** I can do, such that doing it everything else will be easier or unnecessary?

KEY RELATIONSHIPS

How can I improve my key relationships?

For my **key relationships**, what's the **ONE THING** I can do, such that doing it everything else will be easier or unnecessary?

CAREER

How can I improve my career?

For my **career**, what's the **ONE THING** I can do, such that doing it everything else will be easier or unnecessary?

FINANCES

How can I improve my finances?

For my **finances**, what's the **ONE THING** I can do, such that doing it everything else will be easier or unnecessary?

IMPROVEMENT SHEET

FIND THE LEAD DOMINO IN ALL AREAS OF YOUR LIFE,
AND WHACK AWAY AT IT UNTIL IT FALLS.

PHYSICAL HEALTH

How can I improve my physical health?

For my **physical health**, what's the **ONE THING** I can do, such that doing it everything else will be easier or unnecessary?

MENTAL HEALTH

How can I improve my mental health?

For my **mental health**, what's the **ONE THING** I can do, such that doing it everything else will be easier or unnecessary?

PERSONAL LIFE

How can I improve my personal life?

For my **personal life**, what's the **ONE THING** I can do, such that doing it everything else will be easier or unnecessary?

KEY RELATIONSHIPS

How can I improve my key relationships?

For my **key relationships**, what's the **ONE THING** I can do, such that doing it everything else will be easier or unnecessary?

CAREER

How can I improve my career?

For my **career**, what's the **ONE THING** I can do, such that doing it everything else will be easier or unnecessary?

FINANCES

How can I improve my finances?

For my **finances**, what's the **ONE THING** I can do, such that doing it everything else will be easier or unnecessary?

IMPROVEMENT SHEET

FIND THE LEAD DOMINO IN ALL AREAS OF YOUR LIFE,
AND WHACK AWAY AT IT UNTIL IT FALLS.

PHYSICAL HEALTH

How can I improve my physical health?

For my **physical health**, what's the **ONE THING** I can do, such that doing it everything else will be easier or unnecessary?

MENTAL HEALTH

How can I improve my mental health?

For my **mental health**, what's the **ONE THING** I can do, such that doing it everything else will be easier or unnecessary?

PERSONAL LIFE

How can I improve my personal life?

For my **personal life**, what's the **ONE THING** I can do, such that doing it everything else will be easier or unnecessary?

KEY RELATIONSHIPS

How can I improve my key relationships?

For my **key relationships**, what's the **ONE THING** I can do, such that doing it everything else will be easier or unnecessary?

CAREER

How can I improve my career?

For my **career**, what's the **ONE THING** I can do, such that doing it everything else will be easier or unnecessary?

FINANCES

How can I improve my finances?

For my **finances**, what's the **ONE THING** I can do, such that doing it everything else will be easier or unnecessary?

IMPROVEMENT SHEET

FIND THE LEAD DOMINO IN ALL AREAS OF YOUR LIFE,
AND WHACK AWAY AT IT UNTIL IT FALLS.

PHYSICAL HEALTH

How can I improve my physical health?

For my **physical health**, what's the **ONE THING** I can do, such that doing it everything else will be easier or unnecessary?

MENTAL HEALTH

How can I improve my mental health?

For my **mental health**, what's the **ONE THING** I can do, such that doing it everything else will be easier or unnecessary?

PERSONAL LIFE

How can I improve my personal life?

For my **personal life**, what's the **ONE THING** I can do, such that doing it everything else will be easier or unnecessary?

KEY RELATIONSHIPS

How can I improve my key relationships?

For my **key relationships**, what's the **ONE THING** I can do, such that doing it everything else will be easier or unnecessary?

CAREER

How can I improve my career?

For my **career**, what's the **ONE THING** I can do, such that doing it everything else will be easier or unnecessary?

FINANCES

How can I improve my finances?

For my **finances**, what's the **ONE THING** I can do, such that doing it everything else will be easier or unnecessary?

IMPROVEMENT SHEET

FIND THE LEAD DOMINO IN ALL AREAS OF YOUR LIFE,
AND WHACK AWAY AT IT UNTIL IT FALLS.

PHYSICAL HEALTH

How can I improve my physical health?

For my **physical health**, what's the **ONE THING** I can do, such that doing it everything else will be easier or unnecessary?

MENTAL HEALTH

How can I improve my mental health?

For my **mental health**, what's the **ONE THING** I can do, such that doing it everything else will be easier or unnecessary?

PERSONAL LIFE

How can I improve my personal life?

For my **personal life**, what's the **ONE THING** I can do, such that doing it everything else will be easier or unnecessary?

KEY RELATIONSHIPS

How can I improve my key relationships?

For my **key relationships**, what's the **ONE THING** I can do, such that doing it everything else will be easier or unnecessary?

CAREER

How can I improve my career?

For my **career**, what's the **ONE THING** I can do, such that doing it everything else will be easier or unnecessary?

FINANCES

How can I improve my finances?

For my **finances**, what's the **ONE THING** I can do, such that doing it everything else will be easier or unnecessary?

IMPROVEMENT SHEET

FIND THE LEAD DOMINO IN ALL AREAS OF YOUR LIFE,
AND WHACK AWAY AT IT UNTIL IT FALLS.

PHYSICAL HEALTH

How can I improve my physical health?

For my **physical health**, what's the **ONE THING** I can do, such that doing it everything else will be easier or unnecessary?

MENTAL HEALTH

How can I improve my mental health?

For my **mental health**, what's the **ONE THING** I can do, such that doing it everything else will be easier or unnecessary?

PERSONAL LIFE

How can I improve my personal life?

For my **personal life**, what's the **ONE THING** I can do, such that doing it everything else will be easier or unnecessary?

KEY RELATIONSHIPS

How can I improve my key relationships?

For my **key relationships**, what's the **ONE THING** I can do, such that doing it everything else will be easier or unnecessary?

CAREER

How can I improve my career?

For my **career**, what's the **ONE THING** I can do, such that doing it everything else will be easier or unnecessary?

FINANCES

How can I improve my finances?

For my **finances**, what's the **ONE THING** I can do, such that doing it everything else will be easier or unnecessary?

IMPROVEMENT SHEET

FIND THE LEAD DOMINO IN ALL AREAS OF YOUR LIFE,
AND WHACK AWAY AT IT UNTIL IT FALLS.

PHYSICAL HEALTH

How can I improve my physical health?

For my **physical health**, what's the **ONE THING** I can do, such that doing it everything else will be easier or unnecessary?

MENTAL HEALTH

How can I improve my mental health?

For my **mental health**, what's the **ONE THING** I can do, such that doing it everything else will be easier or unnecessary?

PERSONAL LIFE

How can I improve my personal life?

For my **personal life**, what's the **ONE THING** I can do, such that doing it everything else will be easier or unnecessary?

KEY RELATIONSHIPS

How can I improve my key relationships?

For my **key relationships**, what's the **ONE THING** I can do, such that doing it everything else will be easier or unnecessary?

CAREER

How can I improve my career?

For my **career**, what's the **ONE THING** I can do, such that doing it everything else will be easier or unnecessary?

FINANCES

How can I improve my finances?

For my **finances**, what's the **ONE THING** I can do, such that doing it everything else will be easier or unnecessary?

IMPROVEMENT SHEET

FIND THE LEAD DOMINO IN ALL AREAS OF YOUR LIFE,
AND WHACK AWAY AT IT UNTIL IT FALLS.

PHYSICAL HEALTH

How can I improve my physical health?

For my **physical health**, what's the **ONE THING** I can do, such that doing it everything else will be easier or unnecessary?

MENTAL HEALTH

How can I improve my mental health?

For my **mental health**, what's the **ONE THING** I can do, such that doing it everything else will be easier or unnecessary?

PERSONAL LIFE

How can I improve my personal life?

For my **personal life**, what's the **ONE THING** I can do, such that doing it everything else will be easier or unnecessary?

KEY RELATIONSHIPS

How can I improve my key relationships?

For my **key relationships**, what's the **ONE THING** I can do, such that doing it everything else will be easier or unnecessary?

CAREER

How can I improve my career?

For my **career**, what's the **ONE THING** I can do, such that doing it everything else will be easier or unnecessary?

FINANCES

How can I improve my finances?

For my **finances**, what's the **ONE THING** I can do, such that doing it everything else will be easier or unnecessary?

IMPROVEMENT SHEET

FIND THE LEAD DOMINO IN ALL AREAS OF YOUR LIFE,
AND WHACK AWAY AT IT UNTIL IT FALLS.

PHYSICAL HEALTH

How can I improve my physical health?

For my **physical health**, what's the **ONE THING** I can do, such that doing it everything else will be easier or unnecessary?

MENTAL HEALTH

How can I improve my mental health?

For my **mental health**, what's the **ONE THING** I can do, such that doing it everything else will be easier or unnecessary?

PERSONAL LIFE

How can I improve my personal life?

For my **personal life**, what's the **ONE THING** I can do, such that doing it everything else will be easier or unnecessary?

KEY RELATIONSHIPS

How can I improve my key relationships?

For my **key relationships**, what's the **ONE THING** I can do, such that doing it everything else will be easier or unnecessary?

CAREER

How can I improve my career?

For my **career**, what's the **ONE THING** I can do, such that doing it everything else will be easier or unnecessary?

FINANCES

How can I improve my finances?

For my **finances**, what's the **ONE THING** I can do, such that doing it everything else will be easier or unnecessary?

IMPROVEMENT SHEET

FIND THE LEAD DOMINO IN ALL AREAS OF YOUR LIFE,
AND WHACK AWAY AT IT UNTIL IT FALLS.

PHYSICAL HEALTH

How can I improve my physical health?

For my **physical health**, what's the **ONE THING** I can do, such that doing it everything else will be easier or unnecessary?

MENTAL HEALTH

How can I improve my mental health?

For my **mental health**, what's the **ONE THING** I can do, such that doing it everything else will be easier or unnecessary?

PERSONAL LIFE

How can I improve my personal life?

For my **personal life**, what's the **ONE THING** I can do, such that doing it everything else will be easier or unnecessary?

KEY RELATIONSHIPS

How can I improve my key relationships?

For my **key relationships**, what's the **ONE THING** I can do, such that doing it everything else will be easier or unnecessary?

CAREER

How can I improve my career?

For my **career**, what's the **ONE THING** I can do, such that doing it everything else will be easier or unnecessary?

FINANCES

How can I improve my finances?

For my **finances**, what's the **ONE THING** I can do, such that doing it everything else will be easier or unnecessary?

IMPROVEMENT SHEET

FIND THE LEAD DOMINO IN ALL AREAS OF YOUR LIFE,
AND WHACK AWAY AT IT UNTIL IT FALLS.

PHYSICAL HEALTH

How can I improve my physical health?

For my **physical health**, what's the **ONE THING** I can do, such that doing it everything else will be easier or unnecessary?

MENTAL HEALTH

How can I improve my mental health?

For my **mental health**, what's the **ONE THING** I can do, such that doing it everything else will be easier or unnecessary?

PERSONAL LIFE

How can I improve my personal life?

For my **personal life**, what's the **ONE THING** I can do, such that doing it everything else will be easier or unnecessary?

KEY RELATIONSHIPS

How can I improve my key relationships?

For my **key relationships**, what's the **ONE THING** I can do, such that doing it everything else will be easier or unnecessary?

CAREER

How can I improve my career?

For my **career**, what's the **ONE THING** I can do, such that doing it everything else will be easier or unnecessary?

FINANCES

How can I improve my finances?

For my **finances**, what's the **ONE THING** I can do, such that doing it everything else will be easier or unnecessary?

IMPROVEMENT SHEET

FIND THE LEAD DOMINO IN ALL AREAS OF YOUR LIFE,
AND WHACK AWAY AT IT UNTIL IT FALLS.

PHYSICAL HEALTH

How can I improve my physical health?

For my **physical health**, what's the **ONE THING** I can do, such that doing it everything else will be easier or unnecessary?

MENTAL HEALTH

How can I improve my mental health?

For my **mental health**, what's the **ONE THING** I can do, such that doing it everything else will be easier or unnecessary?

PERSONAL LIFE

How can I improve my personal life?

For my **personal life**, what's the **ONE THING** I can do, such that doing it everything else will be easier or unnecessary?

KEY RELATIONSHIPS

How can I improve my key relationships?

For my **key relationships**, what's the **ONE THING** I can do, such that doing it everything else will be easier or unnecessary?

CAREER

How can I improve my career?

For my **career**, what's the **ONE THING** I can do, such that doing it everything else will be easier or unnecessary?

FINANCES

How can I improve my finances?

For my **finances**, what's the **ONE THING** I can do, such that doing it everything else will be easier or unnecessary?

IMPROVEMENT SHEET

FIND THE LEAD DOMINO IN ALL AREAS OF YOUR LIFE,
AND WHACK AWAY AT IT UNTIL IT FALLS.

PHYSICAL HEALTH

How can I improve my physical health?

For my **physical health**, what's the **ONE THING** I can do, such that doing it everything else will be easier or unnecessary?

MENTAL HEALTH

How can I improve my mental health?

For my **mental health**, what's the **ONE THING** I can do, such that doing it everything else will be easier or unnecessary?

PERSONAL LIFE

How can I improve my personal life?

For my **personal life**, what's the **ONE THING** I can do, such that doing it everything else will be easier or unnecessary?

KEY RELATIONSHIPS

How can I improve my key relationships?

For my **key relationships**, what's the **ONE THING** I can do, such that doing it everything else will be easier or unnecessary?

CAREER

How can I improve my career?

For my **career**, what's the **ONE THING** I can do, such that doing it everything else will be easier or unnecessary?

FINANCES

How can I improve my finances?

For my **finances**, what's the **ONE THING** I can do, such that doing it everything else will be easier or unnecessary?

IMPROVEMENT SHEET

FIND THE LEAD DOMINO IN ALL AREAS OF YOUR LIFE,
AND WHACK AWAY AT IT UNTIL IT FALLS.

PHYSICAL HEALTH

How can I improve my physical health?

For my **physical health**, what's the **ONE THING** I can do, such that doing it everything else will be easier or unnecessary?

MENTAL HEALTH

How can I improve my mental health?

For my **mental health**, what's the **ONE THING** I can do, such that doing it everything else will be easier or unnecessary?

PERSONAL LIFE

How can I improve my personal life?

For my **personal life**, what's the **ONE THING** I can do, such that doing it everything else will be easier or unnecessary?

KEY RELATIONSHIPS

How can I improve my key relationships?

For my **key relationships**, what's the **ONE THING** I can do, such that doing it everything else will be easier or unnecessary?

CAREER

How can I improve my career?

For my **career**, what's the **ONE THING** I can do, such that doing it everything else will be easier or unnecessary?

FINANCES

How can I improve my finances?

For my **finances**, what's the **ONE THING** I can do, such that doing it everything else will be easier or unnecessary?

IMPROVEMENT SHEET

FIND THE LEAD DOMINO IN ALL AREAS OF YOUR LIFE,
AND WHACK AWAY AT IT UNTIL IT FALLS.

PHYSICAL HEALTH

How can I improve my physical health?

For my **physical health**, what's the **ONE THING** I can do, such that doing it everything else will be easier or unnecessary?

MENTAL HEALTH

How can I improve my mental health?

For my **mental health**, what's the **ONE THING** I can do, such that doing it everything else will be easier or unnecessary?

PERSONAL LIFE

How can I improve my personal life?

For my **personal life**, what's the **ONE THING** I can do, such that doing it everything else will be easier or unnecessary?

KEY RELATIONSHIPS

How can I improve my key relationships?

For my **key relationships**, what's the **ONE THING** I can do, such that doing it everything else will be easier or unnecessary?

CAREER

How can I improve my career?

For my **career**, what's the **ONE THING** I can do, such that doing it everything else will be easier or unnecessary?

FINANCES

How can I improve my finances?

For my **finances**, what's the **ONE THING** I can do, such that doing it everything else will be easier or unnecessary?

IMPROVEMENT SHEET

FIND THE LEAD DOMINO IN ALL AREAS OF YOUR LIFE,
AND WHACK AWAY AT IT UNTIL IT FALLS.

PHYSICAL HEALTH

How can I improve my physical health?

For my **physical health**, what's the **ONE THING** I can do, such that doing it everything else will be easier or unnecessary?

MENTAL HEALTH

How can I improve my mental health?

For my **mental health**, what's the **ONE THING** I can do, such that doing it everything else will be easier or unnecessary?

PERSONAL LIFE

How can I improve my personal life?

For my **personal life**, what's the **ONE THING** I can do, such that doing it everything else will be easier or unnecessary?

KEY RELATIONSHIPS

How can I improve my key relationships?

For my **key relationships**, what's the **ONE THING** I can do, such that doing it everything else will be easier or unnecessary?

CAREER

How can I improve my career?

For my **career**, what's the **ONE THING** I can do, such that doing it everything else will be easier or unnecessary?

FINANCES

How can I improve my finances?

For my **finances**, what's the **ONE THING** I can do, such that doing it everything else will be easier or unnecessary?

IMPROVEMENT SHEET

FIND THE LEAD DOMINO IN ALL AREAS OF YOUR LIFE,
AND WHACK AWAY AT IT UNTIL IT FALLS.

PHYSICAL HEALTH

How can I improve my physical health?

For my **physical health**, what's the **ONE THING** I can do, such that doing it everything else will be easier or unnecessary?

MENTAL HEALTH

How can I improve my mental health?

For my **mental health**, what's the **ONE THING** I can do, such that doing it everything else will be easier or unnecessary?

PERSONAL LIFE

How can I improve my personal life?

For my **personal life**, what's the **ONE THING** I can do, such that doing it everything else will be easier or unnecessary?

KEY RELATIONSHIPS

How can I improve my key relationships?

For my **key relationships**, what's the **ONE THING** I can do, such that doing it everything else will be easier or unnecessary?

CAREER

How can I improve my career?

For my **career**, what's the **ONE THING** I can do, such that doing it everything else will be easier or unnecessary?

FINANCES

How can I improve my finances?

For my **finances**, what's the **ONE THING** I can do, such that doing it everything else will be easier or unnecessary?

IMPROVEMENT SHEET

FIND THE LEAD DOMINO IN ALL AREAS OF YOUR LIFE,
AND WHACK AWAY AT IT UNTIL IT FALLS.

PHYSICAL HEALTH

How can I improve my physical health?

For my **physical health**, what's the **ONE THING** I can do, such that doing it everything else will be easier or unnecessary?

MENTAL HEALTH

How can I improve my mental health?

For my **mental health**, what's the **ONE THING** I can do, such that doing it everything else will be easier or unnecessary?

PERSONAL LIFE

How can I improve my personal life?

For my **personal life**, what's the **ONE THING** I can do, such that doing it everything else will be easier or unnecessary?

KEY RELATIONSHIPS

How can I improve my key relationships?

For my **key relationships**, what's the **ONE THING** I can do, such that doing it everything else will be easier or unnecessary?

CAREER

How can I improve my career?

For my **career**, what's the **ONE THING** I can do, such that doing it everything else will be easier or unnecessary?

FINANCES

How can I improve my finances?

For my **finances**, what's the **ONE THING** I can do, such that doing it everything else will be easier or unnecessary?

IMPROVEMENT SHEET

FIND THE LEAD DOMINO IN ALL AREAS OF YOUR LIFE,
AND WHACK AWAY AT IT UNTIL IT FALLS.

PHYSICAL HEALTH

How can I improve my physical health?

For my **physical health**, what's the **ONE THING** I can do, such that doing it everything else will be easier or unnecessary?

MENTAL HEALTH

How can I improve my mental health?

For my **mental health**, what's the **ONE THING** I can do, such that doing it everything else will be easier or unnecessary?

PERSONAL LIFE

How can I improve my personal life?

For my **personal life**, what's the **ONE THING** I can do, such that doing it everything else will be easier or unnecessary?

KEY RELATIONSHIPS

How can I improve my key relationships?

For my **key relationships**, what's the **ONE THING** I can do, such that doing it everything else will be easier or unnecessary?

CAREER

How can I improve my career?

For my **career**, what's the **ONE THING** I can do, such that doing it everything else will be easier or unnecessary?

FINANCES

How can I improve my finances?

For my **finances**, what's the **ONE THING** I can do, such that doing it everything else will be easier or unnecessary?

IMPROVEMENT SHEET

FIND THE LEAD DOMINO IN ALL AREAS OF YOUR LIFE,
AND WHACK AWAY AT IT UNTIL IT FALLS.

PHYSICAL HEALTH

How can I improve my physical health?

For my **physical health**, what's the **ONE THING** I can do, such that doing it everything else will be easier or unnecessary?

MENTAL HEALTH

How can I improve my mental health?

For my **mental health**, what's the **ONE THING** I can do, such that doing it everything else will be easier or unnecessary?

PERSONAL LIFE

How can I improve my personal life?

For my **personal life**, what's the **ONE THING** I can do, such that doing it everything else will be easier or unnecessary?

KEY RELATIONSHIPS

How can I improve my key relationships?

For my **key relationships**, what's the **ONE THING** I can do, such that doing it everything else will be easier or unnecessary?

CAREER

How can I improve my career?

For my **career**, what's the **ONE THING** I can do, such that doing it everything else will be easier or unnecessary?

FINANCES

How can I improve my finances?

For my **finances**, what's the **ONE THING** I can do, such that doing it everything else will be easier or unnecessary?

IMPROVEMENT SHEET

FIND THE LEAD DOMINO IN ALL AREAS OF YOUR LIFE,
AND WHACK AWAY AT IT UNTIL IT FALLS.

PHYSICAL HEALTH

How can I improve my physical health?

For my **physical health**, what's the **ONE THING** I can do, such that doing it everything else will be easier or unnecessary?

MENTAL HEALTH

How can I improve my mental health?

For my **mental health**, what's the **ONE THING** I can do, such that doing it everything else will be easier or unnecessary?

PERSONAL LIFE

How can I improve my personal life?

For my **personal life**, what's the **ONE THING** I can do, such that doing it everything else will be easier or unnecessary?

KEY RELATIONSHIPS

How can I improve my key relationships?

For my **key relationships**, what's the **ONE THING** I can do, such that doing it everything else will be easier or unnecessary?

CAREER

How can I improve my career?

For my **career**, what's the **ONE THING** I can do, such that doing it everything else will be easier or unnecessary?

FINANCES

How can I improve my finances?

For my **finances**, what's the **ONE THING** I can do, such that doing it everything else will be easier or unnecessary?

IMPROVEMENT SHEET

FIND THE LEAD DOMINO IN ALL AREAS OF YOUR LIFE,
AND WHACK AWAY AT IT UNTIL IT FALLS.

PHYSICAL HEALTH

How can I improve my physical health?

For my **physical health**, what's the **ONE THING** I can do, such that doing it everything else will be easier or unnecessary?

MENTAL HEALTH

How can I improve my mental health?

For my **mental health**, what's the **ONE THING** I can do, such that doing it everything else will be easier or unnecessary?

PERSONAL LIFE

How can I improve my personal life?

For my **personal life**, what's the **ONE THING** I can do, such that doing it everything else will be easier or unnecessary?

KEY RELATIONSHIPS

How can I improve my key relationships?

For my **key relationships**, what's the **ONE THING** I can do, such that doing it everything else will be easier or unnecessary?

CAREER

How can I improve my career?

For my **career**, what's the **ONE THING** I can do, such that doing it everything else will be easier or unnecessary?

FINANCES

How can I improve my finances?

For my **finances**, what's the **ONE THING** I can do, such that doing it everything else will be easier or unnecessary?

IMPROVEMENT SHEET

FIND THE LEAD DOMINO IN ALL AREAS OF YOUR LIFE,
AND WHACK AWAY AT IT UNTIL IT FALLS.

PHYSICAL HEALTH

How can I improve my physical health?

For my **physical health**, what's the **ONE THING** I can do, such that doing it everything else will be easier or unnecessary?

MENTAL HEALTH

How can I improve my mental health?

For my **mental health**, what's the **ONE THING** I can do, such that doing it everything else will be easier or unnecessary?

PERSONAL LIFE

How can I improve my personal life?

For my **personal life**, what's the **ONE THING** I can do, such that doing it everything else will be easier or unnecessary?

KEY RELATIONSHIPS

How can I improve my key relationships?

For my **key relationships**, what's the **ONE THING** I can do, such that doing it everything else will be easier or unnecessary?

CAREER

How can I improve my career?

For my **career**, what's the **ONE THING** I can do, such that doing it everything else will be easier or unnecessary?

FINANCES

How can I improve my finances?

For my **finances**, what's the **ONE THING** I can do, such that doing it everything else will be easier or unnecessary?

IMPROVEMENT SHEET

FIND THE LEAD DOMINO IN ALL AREAS OF YOUR LIFE,
AND WHACK AWAY AT IT UNTIL IT FALLS.

PHYSICAL HEALTH

How can I improve my physical health?

For my **physical health**, what's the **ONE THING** I can do, such that doing it everything else will be easier or unnecessary?

MENTAL HEALTH

How can I improve my mental health?

For my **mental health**, what's the **ONE THING** I can do, such that doing it everything else will be easier or unnecessary?

PERSONAL LIFE

How can I improve my personal life?

For my **personal life**, what's the **ONE THING** I can do, such that doing it everything else will be easier or unnecessary?

KEY RELATIONSHIPS

How can I improve my key relationships?

For my **key relationships**, what's the **ONE THING** I can do, such that doing it everything else will be easier or unnecessary?

CAREER

How can I improve my career?

For my **career**, what's the **ONE THING** I can do, such that doing it everything else will be easier or unnecessary?

FINANCES

How can I improve my finances?

For my **finances**, what's the **ONE THING** I can do, such that doing it everything else will be easier or unnecessary?

IMPROVEMENT SHEET

FIND THE LEAD DOMINO IN ALL AREAS OF YOUR LIFE,
AND WHACK AWAY AT IT UNTIL IT FALLS.

PHYSICAL HEALTH

How can I improve my physical health?

For my **physical health**, what's the **ONE THING** I can do, such that doing it everything else will be easier or unnecessary?

MENTAL HEALTH

How can I improve my mental health?

For my **mental health**, what's the **ONE THING** I can do, such that doing it everything else will be easier or unnecessary?

PERSONAL LIFE

How can I improve my personal life?

For my **personal life**, what's the **ONE THING** I can do, such that doing it everything else will be easier or unnecessary?

KEY RELATIONSHIPS

How can I improve my key relationships?

For my **key relationships**, what's the **ONE THING** I can do, such that doing it everything else will be easier or unnecessary?

CAREER

How can I improve my career?

For my **career**, what's the **ONE THING** I can do, such that doing it everything else will be easier or unnecessary?

FINANCES

How can I improve my finances?

For my **finances**, what's the **ONE THING** I can do, such that doing it everything else will be easier or unnecessary?

IMPROVEMENT SHEET

FIND THE LEAD DOMINO IN ALL AREAS OF YOUR LIFE,
AND WHACK AWAY AT IT UNTIL IT FALLS.

PHYSICAL HEALTH

How can I improve my physical health?

For my **physical health**, what's the **ONE THING** I can do, such that doing it everything else will be easier or unnecessary?

MENTAL HEALTH

How can I improve my mental health?

For my **mental health**, what's the **ONE THING** I can do, such that doing it everything else will be easier or unnecessary?

PERSONAL LIFE

How can I improve my personal life?

For my **personal life**, what's the **ONE THING** I can do, such that doing it everything else will be easier or unnecessary?

KEY RELATIONSHIPS

How can I improve my key relationships?

For my **key relationships**, what's the **ONE THING** I can do, such that doing it everything else will be easier or unnecessary?

CAREER

How can I improve my career?

For my **career**, what's the **ONE THING** I can do, such that doing it everything else will be easier or unnecessary?

FINANCES

How can I improve my finances?

For my **finances**, what's the **ONE THING** I can do, such that doing it everything else will be easier or unnecessary?

IMPROVEMENT SHEET

FIND THE LEAD DOMINO IN ALL AREAS OF YOUR LIFE,
AND WHACK AWAY AT IT UNTIL IT FALLS.

PHYSICAL HEALTH

How can I improve my physical health?

For my **physical health**, what's the **ONE THING** I can do, such that doing it everything else will be easier or unnecessary?

MENTAL HEALTH

How can I improve my mental health?

For my **mental health**, what's the **ONE THING** I can do, such that doing it everything else will be easier or unnecessary?

PERSONAL LIFE

How can I improve my personal life?

For my **personal life**, what's the **ONE THING** I can do, such that doing it everything else will be easier or unnecessary?

KEY RELATIONSHIPS

How can I improve my key relationships?

For my **key relationships**, what's the **ONE THING** I can do, such that doing it everything else will be easier or unnecessary?

CAREER

How can I improve my career?

For my **career**, what's the **ONE THING** I can do, such that doing it everything else will be easier or unnecessary?

FINANCES

How can I improve my finances?

For my **finances**, what's the **ONE THING** I can do, such that doing it everything else will be easier or unnecessary?

IMPROVEMENT SHEET

FIND THE LEAD DOMINO IN ALL AREAS OF YOUR LIFE,
AND WHACK AWAY AT IT UNTIL IT FALLS.

PHYSICAL HEALTH

How can I improve my physical health?

For my **physical health**, what's the **ONE THING** I can do, such that doing it everything else will be easier or unnecessary?

MENTAL HEALTH

How can I improve my mental health?

For my **mental health**, what's the **ONE THING** I can do, such that doing it everything else will be easier or unnecessary?

PERSONAL LIFE

How can I improve my personal life?

For my **personal life**, what's the **ONE THING** I can do, such that doing it everything else will be easier or unnecessary?

KEY RELATIONSHIPS

How can I improve my key relationships?

For my **key relationships**, what's the **ONE THING** I can do, such that doing it everything else will be easier or unnecessary?

CAREER

How can I improve my career?

For my **career**, what's the **ONE THING** I can do, such that doing it everything else will be easier or unnecessary?

FINANCES

How can I improve my finances?

For my **finances**, what's the **ONE THING** I can do, such that doing it everything else will be easier or unnecessary?

IMPROVEMENT SHEET

FIND THE LEAD DOMINO IN ALL AREAS OF YOUR LIFE,
AND WHACK AWAY AT IT UNTIL IT FALLS.

PHYSICAL HEALTH

How can I improve my physical health?

For my **physical health**, what's the **ONE THING** I can do, such that doing it everything else will be easier or unnecessary?

MENTAL HEALTH

How can I improve my mental health?

For my **mental health**, what's the **ONE THING** I can do, such that doing it everything else will be easier or unnecessary?

PERSONAL LIFE

How can I improve my personal life?

For my **personal life**, what's the **ONE THING** I can do, such that doing it everything else will be easier or unnecessary?

KEY RELATIONSHIPS

How can I improve my key relationships?

For my **key relationships**, what's the **ONE THING** I can do, such that doing it everything else will be easier or unnecessary?

CAREER

How can I improve my career?

For my **career**, what's the **ONE THING** I can do, such that doing it everything else will be easier or unnecessary?

FINANCES

How can I improve my finances?

For my **finances**, what's the **ONE THING** I can do, such that doing it everything else will be easier or unnecessary?

IMPROVEMENT SHEET

FIND THE LEAD DOMINO IN ALL AREAS OF YOUR LIFE,
AND WHACK AWAY AT IT UNTIL IT FALLS.

PHYSICAL HEALTH

How can I improve my physical health?

For my **physical health**, what's the **ONE THING** I can do, such that doing it everything else will be easier or unnecessary?

MENTAL HEALTH

How can I improve my mental health?

For my **mental health**, what's the **ONE THING** I can do, such that doing it everything else will be easier or unnecessary?

PERSONAL LIFE

How can I improve my personal life?

For my **personal life**, what's the **ONE THING** I can do, such that doing it everything else will be easier or unnecessary?

KEY RELATIONSHIPS

How can I improve my key relationships?

For my **key relationships**, what's the **ONE THING** I can do, such that doing it everything else will be easier or unnecessary?

CAREER

How can I improve my career?

For my **career**, what's the **ONE THING** I can do, such that doing it everything else will be easier or unnecessary?

FINANCES

How can I improve my finances?

For my **finances**, what's the **ONE THING** I can do, such that doing it everything else will be easier or unnecessary?

IMPROVEMENT SHEET

FIND THE LEAD DOMINO IN ALL AREAS OF YOUR LIFE,
AND WHACK AWAY AT IT UNTIL IT FALLS.

PHYSICAL HEALTH

How can I improve my physical health?

For my **physical health**, what's the **ONE THING** I can do, such that doing it everything else will be easier or unnecessary?

MENTAL HEALTH

How can I improve my mental health?

For my **mental health**, what's the **ONE THING** I can do, such that doing it everything else will be easier or unnecessary?

PERSONAL LIFE

How can I improve my personal life?

For my **personal life**, what's the **ONE THING** I can do, such that doing it everything else will be easier or unnecessary?

KEY RELATIONSHIPS

How can I improve my key relationships?

For my **key relationships**, what's the **ONE THING** I can do, such that doing it everything else will be easier or unnecessary?

CAREER

How can I improve my career?

For my **career**, what's the **ONE THING** I can do, such that doing it everything else will be easier or unnecessary?

FINANCES

How can I improve my finances?

For my **finances**, what's the **ONE THING** I can do, such that doing it everything else will be easier or unnecessary?

IMPROVEMENT SHEET

FIND THE LEAD DOMINO IN ALL AREAS OF YOUR LIFE,
AND WHACK AWAY AT IT UNTIL IT FALLS.

PHYSICAL HEALTH

How can I improve my physical health?

For my **physical health**, what's the **ONE THING** I can do, such that doing it everything else will be easier or unnecessary?

MENTAL HEALTH

How can I improve my mental health?

For my **mental health**, what's the **ONE THING** I can do, such that doing it everything else will be easier or unnecessary?

PERSONAL LIFE

How can I improve my personal life?

For my **personal life**, what's the **ONE THING** I can do, such that doing it everything else will be easier or unnecessary?

KEY RELATIONSHIPS

How can I improve my key relationships?

For my **key relationships**, what's the **ONE THING** I can do, such that doing it everything else will be easier or unnecessary?

CAREER

How can I improve my career?

For my **career**, what's the **ONE THING** I can do, such that doing it everything else will be easier or unnecessary?

FINANCES

How can I improve my finances?

For my **finances**, what's the **ONE THING** I can do, such that doing it everything else will be easier or unnecessary?

Q & A SHEET

BIG & BROAD QUESTION	BIG & SPECIFIC QUESTION	SMALL & BROAD QUESTION	SMALL & SPECIFIC QUESTION

"DOABLE"
ANSWER

"STRETCH"
ANSWER

"POSSIBILITY"
ANSWER

THE QUALITY OF ANY ANSWER IS DIRECTLY DETERMINED BY THE QUALITY
OF THE QUESTION.

Q&A SHEET

GREAT QUESTIONS LEAD TO GREAT ANSWERS.
THINK BIG AND SPECIFIC; RESEARCH AND ROLE MODEL.

ASK A GREAT QUESTION

BIG (extreme, ambitious, bold)

BROAD (general, unclear)

SPECIFIC (what, how much, until when)

Big & Broad	**Big & Specific**
What's the ONE THING I can do to...	*What's the ONE THING I can do to...*

Small & Broad	**Small & Specific**
What's the ONE THING I can do to...	*What's the ONE THING I can do to...*

SMALL (reasonable, average, safe)

FIND A GREAT ANSWER

Doable: Within reach of your knowledge, skills, and experience.

Stretch: Still within your reach – the farthest end of your current abilities. Research & study others.

Possibility: Beyond what is already known and being done. Research & study others, then innovate.

DAYDREAMERS PRINT

Q&A SHEET

GREAT QUESTIONS LEAD TO GREAT ANSWERS.
THINK BIG AND SPECIFIC; RESEARCH AND ROLE MODEL.

ASK A GREAT QUESTION

BIG (extreme, ambitious, bold)

BROAD (general, unclear)

Big & Broad

What's the ONE THING I can do to...

Big & Specific

What's the ONE THING I can do to...

SPECIFIC (what, how much, until when)

Small & Broad

What's the ONE THING I can do to...

Small & Specific

What's the ONE THING I can do to...

SMALL (reasonable, average, safe)

FIND A GREAT ANSWER

Doable: Within reach of your knowledge, skills, and experience.

Stretch: Still within your reach – the farthest end of your current abilities. Research & study others.

Possibility: Beyond what is already known and being done. Research & study others, then innovate.

DAYDREAMERS PRINT

Q&A SHEET

GREAT QUESTIONS LEAD TO GREAT ANSWERS.
THINK BIG AND SPECIFIC; RESEARCH AND ROLE MODEL.

ASK A GREAT QUESTION

BIG (extreme, ambitious, bold)

BROAD (general, unclear)

SPECIFIC (what, how much, until when)

Big & Broad
What's the ONE THING I can do to...

Big & Specific
What's the ONE THING I can do to...

Small & Broad
What's the ONE THING I can do to...

Small & Specific
What's the ONE THING I can do to...

SMALL (reasonable, average, safe)

FIND A GREAT ANSWER

Doable: Within reach of your knowledge, skills, and experience.

Stretch: Still within your reach – the farthest end of your current abilities. Research & study others.

Possibility: Beyond what is already known and being done. Research & study others, then innovate.

DAYDREAMERS PRINT

Q&A SHEET

GREAT QUESTIONS LEAD TO GREAT ANSWERS.
THINK BIG AND SPECIFIC; RESEARCH AND ROLE MODEL.

ASK A GREAT QUESTION

BIG (extreme, ambitious, bold)

Big & Broad	**Big & Specific**
What's the ONE THING I can do to...	*What's the ONE THING I can do to...*
Small & Broad	**Small & Specific**
What's the ONE THING I can do to...	*What's the ONE THING I can do to...*

BROAD (general, unclear)

SPECIFIC (what, how much, until when)

SMALL (reasonable, average, safe)

FIND A GREAT ANSWER

Doable: Within reach of your knowledge, skills, and experience.

Stretch: Still within your reach – the farthest end of your current abilities. Research & study others.

Possibility: Beyond what is already known and being done. Research & study others, then innovate.

DAYDREAMERS PRINT

Q&A SHEET

GREAT QUESTIONS LEAD TO GREAT ANSWERS.
THINK BIG AND SPECIFIC; RESEARCH AND ROLE MODEL.

ASK A GREAT QUESTION

BIG (extreme, ambitious, bold)

Big & Broad	**Big & Specific**
What's the ONE THING I can do to...	*What's the ONE THING I can do to...*
Small & Broad	**Small & Specific**
What's the ONE THING I can do to...	*What's the ONE THING I can do to...*

BROAD (general, unclear)

SPECIFIC (what, how much, until when)

SMALL (reasonable, average, safe)

FIND A GREAT ANSWER

Doable: Within reach of your knowledge, skills, and experience.

Stretch: Still within your reach – the farthest end of your current abilities. Research & study others.

Possibility: Beyond what is already known and being done. Research & study others, then innovate.

DAYDREAMERS PRINT

Q&A SHEET

GREAT QUESTIONS LEAD TO GREAT ANSWERS.
THINK BIG AND SPECIFIC; RESEARCH AND ROLE MODEL.

ASK A GREAT QUESTION

BIG (extreme, ambitious, bold)

Big & Broad
What's the ONE THING I can do to...

Big & Specific
What's the ONE THING I can do to...

BROAD (general, unclear)

SPECIFIC (what, how much, until when)

Small & Broad
What's the ONE THING I can do to...

Small & Specific
What's the ONE THING I can do to...

SMALL (reasonable, average, safe)

FIND A GREAT ANSWER

Doable: Within reach of your knowledge, skills, and experience.

Stretch: Still within your reach — the farthest end of your current abilities. Research & study others.

Possibility: Beyond what is already known and being done. Research & study others, then innovate.

Q&A SHEET

GREAT QUESTIONS LEAD TO GREAT ANSWERS.
THINK BIG AND SPECIFIC; RESEARCH AND ROLE MODEL.

ASK A GREAT QUESTION

BIG (extreme, ambitious, bold)

Big & Broad	**Big & Specific**
What's the ONE THING I can do to...	*What's the ONE THING I can do to...*

BROAD (general, unclear)

SPECIFIC (what, how much, until when)

Small & Broad	**Small & Specific**
What's the ONE THING I can do to...	*What's the ONE THING I can do to...*

SMALL (reasonable, average, safe)

FIND A GREAT ANSWER

Doable: Within reach of your knowledge, skills, and experience.

Stretch: Still within your reach – the farthest end of your current abilities. Research & study others.

Possibility: Beyond what is already known and being done. Research & study others, then innovate.

Q&A SHEET

GREAT QUESTIONS LEAD TO GREAT ANSWERS.
THINK BIG AND SPECIFIC; RESEARCH AND ROLE MODEL.

ASK A GREAT QUESTION

BIG (extreme, ambitious, bold)

Big & Broad	**Big & Specific**
What's the ONE THING I can do to...	*What's the ONE THING I can do to...*
Small & Broad	**Small & Specific**
What's the ONE THING I can do to...	*What's the ONE THING I can do to...*

BROAD (general, unclear)

SPECIFIC (what, how much, until when)

SMALL (reasonable, average, safe)

FIND A GREAT ANSWER

Doable: Within reach of your knowledge, skills, and experience.

Stretch: Still within your reach – the farthest end of your current abilities. Research & study others.

Possibility: Beyond what is already known and being done. Research & study others, then innovate.

Q&A SHEET

GREAT QUESTIONS LEAD TO GREAT ANSWERS.
THINK BIG AND SPECIFIC; RESEARCH AND ROLE MODEL.

ASK A GREAT QUESTION

BIG (extreme, ambitious, bold)

Big & Broad	**Big & Specific**
What's the ONE THING I can do to...	*What's the ONE THING I can do to...*

BROAD (general, unclear) — **SPECIFIC (what, how much, until when)**

Small & Broad	**Small & Specific**
What's the ONE THING I can do to...	*What's the ONE THING I can do to...*

SMALL (reasonable, average, safe)

FIND A GREAT ANSWER

Doable: Within reach of your knowledge, skills, and experience.

Stretch: Still within your reach – the farthest end of your current abilities. Research & study others.

Possibility: Beyond what is already known and being done. Research & study others, then innovate.

Q&A SHEET

GREAT QUESTIONS LEAD TO GREAT ANSWERS.
THINK BIG AND SPECIFIC; RESEARCH AND ROLE MODEL.

ASK A GREAT QUESTION

BIG (extreme, ambitious, bold)

Big & Broad	**Big & Specific**
What's the ONE THING I can do to...	*What's the ONE THING I can do to...*

BROAD (general, unclear)

SPECIFIC (what, how much, until when)

Small & Broad	**Small & Specific**
What's the ONE THING I can do to...	*What's the ONE THING I can do to...*

SMALL (reasonable, average, safe)

FIND A GREAT ANSWER

Doable: Within reach of your knowledge, skills, and experience.

Stretch: Still within your reach — the farthest end of your current abilities. Research & study others.

Possibility: Beyond what is already known and being done. Research & study others, then innovate.

DAYDREAMERS PRINT

Q&A SHEET

GREAT QUESTIONS LEAD TO GREAT ANSWERS.
THINK BIG AND SPECIFIC; RESEARCH AND ROLE MODEL.

ASK A GREAT QUESTION

BIG (extreme, ambitious, bold)

BROAD (general, unclear)

SPECIFIC (what, how much, until when)

Big & Broad
What's the ONE THING I can do to...

Big & Specific
What's the ONE THING I can do to...

Small & Broad
What's the ONE THING I can do to...

Small & Specific
What's the ONE THING I can do to...

SMALL (reasonable, average, safe)

FIND A GREAT ANSWER

Doable: Within reach of your knowledge, skills, and experience.

Stretch: Still within your reach – the farthest end of your current abilities. Research & study others.

Possibility: Beyond what is already known and being done. Research & study others, then innovate.

DAYDREAMERS PRINT

Q&A SHEET

GREAT QUESTIONS LEAD TO GREAT ANSWERS.
THINK BIG AND SPECIFIC; RESEARCH AND ROLE MODEL.

ASK A GREAT QUESTION

BIG (extreme, ambitious, bold)

Big & Broad	**Big & Specific**
What's the ONE THING I can do to...	*What's the ONE THING I can do to...*

BROAD (general, unclear)

SPECIFIC (what, how much, until when)

Small & Broad	**Small & Specific**
What's the ONE THING I can do to...	*What's the ONE THING I can do to...*

SMALL (reasonable, average, safe)

FIND A GREAT ANSWER

Doable: Within reach of your knowledge, skills, and experience.

Stretch: Still within your reach – the farthest end of your current abilities. Research & study others.

Possibility: Beyond what is already known and being done. Research & study others, then innovate.

DAYDREAMERS PRINT

Q&A SHEET

GREAT QUESTIONS LEAD TO GREAT ANSWERS.
THINK BIG AND SPECIFIC; RESEARCH AND ROLE MODEL.

ASK A GREAT QUESTION

BIG (extreme, ambitious, bold)

Big & Broad	**Big & Specific**
What's the ONE THING I can do to...	*What's the ONE THING I can do to...*

BROAD (general, unclear) · **SPECIFIC (what, how much, until when)**

Small & Broad	**Small & Specific**
What's the ONE THING I can do to...	*What's the ONE THING I can do to...*

SMALL (reasonable, average, safe)

FIND A GREAT ANSWER

Doable: Within reach of your knowledge, skills, and experience.

Stretch: Still within your reach – the farthest end of your current abilities. Research & study others.

Possibility: Beyond what is already known and being done. Research & study others, then innovate.

Q&A SHEET

GREAT QUESTIONS LEAD TO GREAT ANSWERS.
THINK BIG AND SPECIFIC; RESEARCH AND ROLE MODEL.

ASK A GREAT QUESTION

BIG (extreme, ambitious, bold)

Big & Broad	**Big & Specific**
What's the ONE THING I can do to...	*What's the ONE THING I can do to...*

BROAD (general, unclear) | **SPECIFIC (what, how much, until when)**

Small & Broad	**Small & Specific**
What's the ONE THING I can do to...	*What's the ONE THING I can do to...*

SMALL (reasonable, average, safe)

FIND A GREAT ANSWER

Doable: Within reach of your knowledge, skills, and experience.

Stretch: Still within your reach – the farthest end of your current abilities. Research & study others.

Possibility: Beyond what is already known and being done. Research & study others, then innovate.

DAYDREAMERS PRINT

Q&A SHEET

GREAT QUESTIONS LEAD TO GREAT ANSWERS.
THINK BIG AND SPECIFIC; RESEARCH AND ROLE MODEL.

ASK A GREAT QUESTION

BIG (extreme, ambitious, bold)

Big & Broad	**Big & Specific**
What's the ONE THING I can do to...	*What's the ONE THING I can do to...*

BROAD (general, unclear)

SPECIFIC (what, how much, until when)

Small & Broad	**Small & Specific**
What's the ONE THING I can do to...	*What's the ONE THING I can do to...*

SMALL (reasonable, average, safe)

FIND A GREAT ANSWER

Doable: Within reach of your knowledge, skills, and experience.

Stretch: Still within your reach – the farthest end of your current abilities. Research & study others.

Possibility: Beyond what is already known and being done. Research & study others, then innovate.

Q&A SHEET

GREAT QUESTIONS LEAD TO GREAT ANSWERS.
THINK BIG AND SPECIFIC; RESEARCH AND ROLE MODEL.

ASK A GREAT QUESTION

BIG (extreme, ambitious, bold)

BROAD (general, unclear)

Big & Broad

What's the ONE THING I can do to...

Big & Specific

What's the ONE THING I can do to...

SPECIFIC (what, how much, until when)

Small & Broad

What's the ONE THING I can do to...

Small & Specific

What's the ONE THING I can do to...

SMALL (reasonable, average, safe)

FIND A GREAT ANSWER

Doable: Within reach of your knowledge, skills, and experience.

Stretch: Still within your reach – the farthest end of your current abilities. Research & study others.

Possibility: Beyond what is already known and being done. Research & study others, then innovate.

DAYDREAMERS PRINT

Q&A SHEET

GREAT QUESTIONS LEAD TO GREAT ANSWERS.
THINK BIG AND SPECIFIC; RESEARCH AND ROLE MODEL.

ASK A GREAT QUESTION

BIG (extreme, ambitious, bold)

BROAD (general, unclear)

SPECIFIC (what, how much, until when)

Big & Broad

What's the ONE THING I can do to...

Big & Specific

What's the ONE THING I can do to...

Small & Broad

What's the ONE THING I can do to...

Small & Specific

What's the ONE THING I can do to...

SMALL (reasonable, average, safe)

FIND A GREAT ANSWER

Doable: Within reach of your knowledge, skills, and experience.

Stretch: Still within your reach – the farthest end of your current abilities. Research & study others.

Possibility: Beyond what is already known and being done. Research & study others, then innovate.

Q&A SHEET

GREAT QUESTIONS LEAD TO GREAT ANSWERS.
THINK BIG AND SPECIFIC; RESEARCH AND ROLE MODEL.

ASK A GREAT QUESTION

BIG (extreme, ambitious, bold)

BROAD (general, unclear)

SPECIFIC (what, how much, until when)

Big & Broad
What's the ONE THING I can do to...

Big & Specific
What's the ONE THING I can do to...

Small & Broad
What's the ONE THING I can do to...

Small & Specific
What's the ONE THING I can do to...

SMALL (reasonable, average, safe)

FIND A GREAT ANSWER

Doable: Within reach of your knowledge, skills, and experience.

Stretch: Still within your reach — the farthest end of your current abilities. Research & study others.

Possibility: Beyond what is already known and being done. Research & study others, then innovate.

DAYDREAMERS PRINT

Q&A SHEET

GREAT QUESTIONS LEAD TO GREAT ANSWERS.
THINK BIG AND SPECIFIC; RESEARCH AND ROLE MODEL.

ASK A GREAT QUESTION

BIG (extreme, ambitious, bold)

Big & Broad	**Big & Specific**
What's the ONE THING I can do to...	*What's the ONE THING I can do to...*
Small & Broad	**Small & Specific**
What's the ONE THING I can do to...	*What's the ONE THING I can do to...*

BROAD (general, unclear)

SPECIFIC (what, how much, until when)

SMALL (reasonable, average, safe)

FIND A GREAT ANSWER

Doable: Within reach of your knowledge, skills, and experience.

Stretch: Still within your reach – the farthest end of your current abilities. Research & study others.

Possibility: Beyond what is already known and being done. Research & study others, then innovate.

DAYDREAMERS PRINT

Q&A SHEET

GREAT QUESTIONS LEAD TO GREAT ANSWERS.
THINK BIG AND SPECIFIC; RESEARCH AND ROLE MODEL.

ASK A GREAT QUESTION

BIG (extreme, ambitious, bold)

Big & Broad	**Big & Specific**
What's the ONE THING I can do to...	*What's the ONE THING I can do to...*

BROAD (general, unclear)

SPECIFIC (what, how much, until when)

Small & Broad	**Small & Specific**
What's the ONE THING I can do to...	*What's the ONE THING I can do to...*

SMALL (reasonable, average, safe)

FIND A GREAT ANSWER

Doable: Within reach of your knowledge, skills, and experience.

Stretch: Still within your reach – the farthest end of your current abilities. Research & study others.

Possibility: Beyond what is already known and being done. Research & study others, then innovate.

Q&A SHEET

GREAT QUESTIONS LEAD TO GREAT ANSWERS.
THINK BIG AND SPECIFIC; RESEARCH AND ROLE MODEL.

ASK A GREAT QUESTION

BIG (extreme, ambitious, bold)

BROAD (general, unclear)

Big & Broad
What's the ONE THING I can do to...

Big & Specific
What's the ONE THING I can do to...

SPECIFIC (what, how much, until when)

Small & Broad
What's the ONE THING I can do to...

Small & Specific
What's the ONE THING I can do to...

SMALL (reasonable, average, safe)

FIND A GREAT ANSWER

Doable: Within reach of your knowledge, skills, and experience.

Stretch: Still within your reach – the farthest end of your current abilities. Research & study others.

Possibility: Beyond what is already known and being done. Research & study others, then innovate.

Q&A SHEET

GREAT QUESTIONS LEAD TO GREAT ANSWERS.
THINK BIG AND SPECIFIC; RESEARCH AND ROLE MODEL.

ASK A GREAT QUESTION

BIG (extreme, ambitious, bold)

<table>
<tr><td>Big & Broad</td><td>Big & Specific</td></tr>
<tr><td>What's the ONE THING I can do to...</td><td>What's the ONE THING I can do to...</td></tr>
</table>

BROAD (general, unclear)

SPECIFIC (what, how much, until when)

<table>
<tr><td>Small & Broad</td><td>Small & Specific</td></tr>
<tr><td>What's the ONE THING I can do to...</td><td>What's the ONE THING I can do to...</td></tr>
</table>

SMALL (reasonable, average, safe)

FIND A GREAT ANSWER

Doable: Within reach of your knowledge, skills, and experience.

Stretch: Still within your reach — the farthest end of your current abilities. Research & study others.

Possibility: Beyond what is already known and being done. Research & study others, then innovate.

DAYDREAMERS PRINT

Q&A SHEET

GREAT QUESTIONS LEAD TO GREAT ANSWERS.
THINK BIG AND SPECIFIC; RESEARCH AND ROLE MODEL.

ASK A GREAT QUESTION

BIG (extreme, ambitious, bold)

Big & Broad	**Big & Specific**
What's the ONE THING I can do to...	*What's the ONE THING I can do to...*

BROAD (general, unclear)

SPECIFIC (what, how much, until when)

Small & Broad	**Small & Specific**
What's the ONE THING I can do to...	*What's the ONE THING I can do to...*

SMALL (reasonable, average, safe)

FIND A GREAT ANSWER

Doable: Within reach of your knowledge, skills, and experience.

Stretch: Still within your reach – the farthest end of your current abilities. Research & study others.

Possibility: Beyond what is already known and being done. Research & study others, then innovate.

DAYDREAMERS PRINT

Q&A SHEET

GREAT QUESTIONS LEAD TO GREAT ANSWERS.
THINK BIG AND SPECIFIC; RESEARCH AND ROLE MODEL.

ASK A GREAT QUESTION

BIG (extreme, ambitious, bold)

Big & Broad	**Big & Specific**
What's the ONE THING I can do to...	*What's the ONE THING I can do to...*

BROAD (general, unclear)

SPECIFIC (what, how much, until when)

Small & Broad	**Small & Specific**
What's the ONE THING I can do to...	*What's the ONE THING I can do to...*

SMALL (reasonable, average, safe)

FIND A GREAT ANSWER

Doable: Within reach of your knowledge, skills, and experience.

Stretch: Still within your reach – the farthest end of your current abilities. Research & study others.

Possibility: Beyond what is already known and being done. Research & study others, then innovate.

DAYDREAMERS PRINT

Q&A SHEET

GREAT QUESTIONS LEAD TO GREAT ANSWERS.
THINK BIG AND SPECIFIC; RESEARCH AND ROLE MODEL.

ASK A GREAT QUESTION

BIG (extreme, ambitious, bold)

Big & Broad	**Big & Specific**
What's the ONE THING I can do to...	*What's the ONE THING I can do to...*

BROAD (general, unclear)

SPECIFIC (what, how much, until when)

Small & Broad	**Small & Specific**
What's the ONE THING I can do to...	*What's the ONE THING I can do to...*

SMALL (reasonable, average, safe)

FIND A GREAT ANSWER

Doable: Within reach of your knowledge, skills, and experience.

Stretch: Still within your reach – the farthest end of your current abilities. Research & study others.

Possibility: Beyond what is already known and being done. Research & study others, then innovate.

DAYDREAMERS PRINT

Q&A SHEET

GREAT QUESTIONS LEAD TO GREAT ANSWERS.
THINK BIG AND SPECIFIC; RESEARCH AND ROLE MODEL.

ASK A GREAT QUESTION

BIG (extreme, ambitious, bold)

Big & Broad	**Big & Specific**
What's the ONE THING I can do to...	*What's the ONE THING I can do to...*

BROAD (general, unclear)

SPECIFIC (what, how much, until when)

Small & Broad	**Small & Specific**
What's the ONE THING I can do to...	*What's the ONE THING I can do to...*

SMALL (reasonable, average, safe)

FIND A GREAT ANSWER

Doable: Within reach of your knowledge, skills, and experience.

Stretch: Still within your reach – the farthest end of your current abilities. Research & study others.

Possibility: Beyond what is already known and being done. Research & study others, then innovate.

DAYDREAMERS PRINT

Q&A SHEET

GREAT QUESTIONS LEAD TO GREAT ANSWERS.
THINK BIG AND SPECIFIC; RESEARCH AND ROLE MODEL.

ASK A GREAT QUESTION

BIG (extreme, ambitious, bold)

BROAD (general, unclear)

SPECIFIC (what, how much, until when)

Big & Broad	**Big & Specific**
What's the ONE THING I can do to...	*What's the ONE THING I can do to...*

Small & Broad	**Small & Specific**
What's the ONE THING I can do to...	*What's the ONE THING I can do to...*

SMALL (reasonable, average, safe)

FIND A GREAT ANSWER

Doable: Within reach of your knowledge, skills, and experience.

Stretch: Still within your reach – the farthest end of your current abilities. Research & study others.

Possibility: Beyond what is already known and being done. Research & study others, then innovate.

Q&A SHEET

GREAT QUESTIONS LEAD TO GREAT ANSWERS.
THINK BIG AND SPECIFIC; RESEARCH AND ROLE MODEL.

ASK A GREAT QUESTION

BIG (extreme, ambitious, bold)

Big & Broad	**Big & Specific**
What's the ONE THING I can do to...	*What's the ONE THING I can do to...*

BROAD (general, unclear)

SPECIFIC (what, how much, until when)

Small & Broad	**Small & Specific**
What's the ONE THING I can do to...	*What's the ONE THING I can do to...*

SMALL (reasonable, average, safe)

FIND A GREAT ANSWER

Doable: Within reach of your knowledge, skills, and experience.

Stretch: Still within your reach – the farthest end of your current abilities. Research & study others.

Possibility: Beyond what is already known and being done. Research & study others, then innovate.

DAYDREAMERS PRINT

Q&A SHEET

GREAT QUESTIONS LEAD TO GREAT ANSWERS.
THINK BIG AND SPECIFIC; RESEARCH AND ROLE MODEL.

ASK A GREAT QUESTION

BIG (extreme, ambitious, bold)

BROAD (general, unclear)

Big & Broad
What's the ONE THING I can do to...

Big & Specific
What's the ONE THING I can do to...

SPECIFIC (what, how much, until when)

Small & Broad
What's the ONE THING I can do to...

Small & Specific
What's the ONE THING I can do to...

SMALL (reasonable, average, safe)

FIND A GREAT ANSWER

Doable: Within reach of your knowledge, skills, and experience.

Stretch: Still within your reach – the farthest end of your current abilities. Research & study others.

Possibility: Beyond what is already known and being done. Research & study others, then innovate.

DAYDREAMERS PRINT

Q&A SHEET

GREAT QUESTIONS LEAD TO GREAT ANSWERS.
THINK BIG AND SPECIFIC; RESEARCH AND ROLE MODEL.

ASK A GREAT QUESTION

BIG (extreme, ambitious, bold)

BROAD (general, unclear)

SPECIFIC (what, how much, until when)

Big & Broad
What's the ONE THING I can do to...

Big & Specific
What's the ONE THING I can do to...

Small & Broad
What's the ONE THING I can do to...

Small & Specific
What's the ONE THING I can do to...

SMALL (reasonable, average, safe)

FIND A GREAT ANSWER

Doable: Within reach of your knowledge, skills, and experience.

Stretch: Still within your reach – the farthest end of your current abilities. Research & study others.

Possibility: Beyond what is already known and being done. Research & study others, then innovate.

DAYDREAMERS PRINT

Q&A SHEET

GREAT QUESTIONS LEAD TO GREAT ANSWERS.
THINK BIG AND SPECIFIC; RESEARCH AND ROLE MODEL.

ASK A GREAT QUESTION

BIG (extreme, ambitious, bold)

Big & Broad	**Big & Specific**
What's the ONE THING I can do to...	*What's the ONE THING I can do to...*

BROAD (general, unclear)

SPECIFIC (what, how much, until when)

Small & Broad	**Small & Specific**
What's the ONE THING I can do to...	*What's the ONE THING I can do to...*

SMALL (reasonable, average, safe)

FIND A GREAT ANSWER

Doable: Within reach of your knowledge, skills, and experience.

Stretch: Still within your reach – the farthest end of your current abilities. Research & study others.

Possibility: Beyond what is already known and being done. Research & study others, then innovate.

DAYDREAMERS PRINT

Q&A SHEET

GREAT QUESTIONS LEAD TO GREAT ANSWERS.
THINK BIG AND SPECIFIC; RESEARCH AND ROLE MODEL.

ASK A GREAT QUESTION

BIG (extreme, ambitious, bold)

Big & Broad	**Big & Specific**
What's the ONE THING I can do to...	*What's the ONE THING I can do to...*

BROAD (general, unclear)

SPECIFIC (what, how much, until when)

Small & Broad	**Small & Specific**
What's the ONE THING I can do to...	*What's the ONE THING I can do to...*

SMALL (reasonable, average, safe)

FIND A GREAT ANSWER

Doable: Within reach of your knowledge, skills, and experience.

Stretch: Still within your reach – the farthest end of your current abilities. Research & study others.

Possibility: Beyond what is already known and being done. Research & study others, then innovate.

DAYDREAMERS PRINT

Q&A SHEET

GREAT QUESTIONS LEAD TO GREAT ANSWERS.
THINK BIG AND SPECIFIC; RESEARCH AND ROLE MODEL.

ASK A GREAT QUESTION

BIG (extreme, ambitious, bold)

Big & Broad	**Big & Specific**
What's the ONE THING I can do to...	*What's the ONE THING I can do to...*

BROAD (general, unclear)

SPECIFIC (what, how much, until when)

Small & Broad	**Small & Specific**
What's the ONE THING I can do to...	*What's the ONE THING I can do to...*

SMALL (reasonable, average, safe)

FIND A GREAT ANSWER

Doable: Within reach of your knowledge, skills, and experience.

Stretch: Still within your reach – the farthest end of your current abilities. Research & study others.

Possibility: Beyond what is already known and being done. Research & study others, then innovate.

DAYDREAMERS PRINT

Q&A SHEET

GREAT QUESTIONS LEAD TO GREAT ANSWERS.
THINK BIG AND SPECIFIC; RESEARCH AND ROLE MODEL.

ASK A GREAT QUESTION

BIG (extreme, ambitious, bold)

BROAD (general, unclear)

SPECIFIC (what, how much, until when)

Big & Broad

What's the ONE THING I can do to...

Big & Specific

What's the ONE THING I can do to...

Small & Broad

What's the ONE THING I can do to...

Small & Specific

What's the ONE THING I can do to...

SMALL (reasonable, average, safe)

FIND A GREAT ANSWER

Doable: Within reach of your knowledge, skills, and experience.

Stretch: Still within your reach – the farthest end of your current abilities. Research & study others.

Possibility: Beyond what is already known and being done. Research & study others, then innovate.

DAYDREAMERS PRINT

Q&A SHEET

GREAT QUESTIONS LEAD TO GREAT ANSWERS.
THINK BIG AND SPECIFIC; RESEARCH AND ROLE MODEL.

ASK A GREAT QUESTION

BIG (extreme, ambitious, bold)

Big & Broad	**Big & Specific**
What's the ONE THING I can do to...	*What's the ONE THING I can do to...*

BROAD (general, unclear)

SPECIFIC (what, how much, until when)

Small & Broad	**Small & Specific**
What's the ONE THING I can do to...	*What's the ONE THING I can do to...*

SMALL (reasonable, average, safe)

FIND A GREAT ANSWER

Doable: Within reach of your knowledge, skills, and experience.

Stretch: Still within your reach – the farthest end of your current abilities. Research & study others.

Possibility: Beyond what is already known and being done. Research & study others, then innovate.

Q&A SHEET

GREAT QUESTIONS LEAD TO GREAT ANSWERS.
THINK BIG AND SPECIFIC; RESEARCH AND ROLE MODEL.

ASK A GREAT QUESTION

BIG (extreme, ambitious, bold)

BROAD (general, unclear)

SPECIFIC (what, how much, until when)

Big & Broad
What's the ONE THING I can do to...

Big & Specific
What's the ONE THING I can do to...

Small & Broad
What's the ONE THING I can do to...

Small & Specific
What's the ONE THING I can do to...

SMALL (reasonable, average, safe)

FIND A GREAT ANSWER

Doable: Within reach of your knowledge, skills, and experience.

Stretch: Still within your reach – the farthest end of your current abilities. Research & study others.

Possibility: Beyond what is already known and being done. Research & study others, then innovate.

DAYDREAMERS PRINT

Q&A SHEET

GREAT QUESTIONS LEAD TO GREAT ANSWERS.
THINK BIG AND SPECIFIC; RESEARCH AND ROLE MODEL.

ASK A GREAT QUESTION

BIG (extreme, ambitious, bold)

Big & Broad	**Big & Specific**
What's the ONE THING I can do to...	*What's the ONE THING I can do to...*

BROAD (general, unclear)

SPECIFIC (what, how much, until when)

Small & Broad	**Small & Specific**
What's the ONE THING I can do to...	*What's the ONE THING I can do to...*

SMALL (reasonable, average, safe)

FIND A GREAT ANSWER

Doable: Within reach of your knowledge, skills, and experience.

Stretch: Still within your reach – the farthest end of your current abilities. Research & study others.

Possibility: Beyond what is already known and being done. Research & study others, then innovate.

Q&A SHEET

GREAT QUESTIONS LEAD TO GREAT ANSWERS.
THINK BIG AND SPECIFIC; RESEARCH AND ROLE MODEL.

ASK A GREAT QUESTION

BIG (extreme, ambitious, bold)

Big & Broad	**Big & Specific**
What's the ONE THING I can do to...	*What's the ONE THING I can do to...*

BROAD (general, unclear)

SPECIFIC (what, how much, until when)

Small & Broad	**Small & Specific**
What's the ONE THING I can do to...	*What's the ONE THING I can do to...*

SMALL (reasonable, average, safe)

FIND A GREAT ANSWER

Doable: Within reach of your knowledge, skills, and experience.

Stretch: Still within your reach – the farthest end of your current abilities. Research & study others.

Possibility: Beyond what is already known and being done. Research & study others, then innovate.

DAYDREAMERS PRINT

Q&A SHEET

GREAT QUESTIONS LEAD TO GREAT ANSWERS.
THINK BIG AND SPECIFIC; RESEARCH AND ROLE MODEL.

ASK A GREAT QUESTION

BIG (extreme, ambitious, bold)

Big & Broad	**Big & Specific**
What's the ONE THING I can do to...	*What's the ONE THING I can do to...*

BROAD (general, unclear)

SPECIFIC (what, how much, until when)

Small & Broad	**Small & Specific**
What's the ONE THING I can do to...	*What's the ONE THING I can do to...*

SMALL (reasonable, average, safe)

FIND A GREAT ANSWER

Doable: Within reach of your knowledge, skills, and experience.

Stretch: Still within your reach – the farthest end of your current abilities. Research & study others.

Possibility: Beyond what is already known and being done. Research & study others, then innovate.

DAYDREAMERS PRINT

Q&A SHEET

GREAT QUESTIONS LEAD TO GREAT ANSWERS.
THINK BIG AND SPECIFIC; RESEARCH AND ROLE MODEL.

ASK A GREAT QUESTION

BIG (extreme, ambitious, bold)

Big & Broad	**Big & Specific**
What's the ONE THING I can do to...	*What's the ONE THING I can do to...*
Small & Broad	**Small & Specific**
What's the ONE THING I can do to...	*What's the ONE THING I can do to...*

BROAD (general, unclear)

SPECIFIC (what, how much, until when)

SMALL (reasonable, average, safe)

FIND A GREAT ANSWER

Doable: Within reach of your knowledge, skills, and experience.

Stretch: Still within your reach – the farthest end of your current abilities. Research & study others.

Possibility: Beyond what is already known and being done. Research & study others, then innovate.

DAYDREAMERS PRINT

Q&A SHEET

GREAT QUESTIONS LEAD TO GREAT ANSWERS.
THINK BIG AND SPECIFIC; RESEARCH AND ROLE MODEL.

ASK A GREAT QUESTION

BIG (extreme, ambitious, bold)

BROAD (general, unclear)

SPECIFIC (what, how much, until when)

Big & Broad
What's the ONE THING I can do to...

Big & Specific
What's the ONE THING I can do to...

Small & Broad
What's the ONE THING I can do to...

Small & Specific
What's the ONE THING I can do to...

SMALL (reasonable, average, safe)

FIND A GREAT ANSWER

Doable: Within reach of your knowledge, skills, and experience.

Stretch: Still within your reach – the farthest end of your current abilities. Research & study others.

Possibility: Beyond what is already known and being done. Research & study others, then innovate.

DAYDREAMERS PRINT

Q&A SHEET

GREAT QUESTIONS LEAD TO GREAT ANSWERS.
THINK BIG AND SPECIFIC; RESEARCH AND ROLE MODEL.

ASK A GREAT QUESTION

BIG (extreme, ambitious, bold)

BROAD (general, unclear)

SPECIFIC (what, how much, until when)

Big & Broad

What's the ONE THING I can do to...

Big & Specific

What's the ONE THING I can do to...

Small & Broad

What's the ONE THING I can do to...

Small & Specific

What's the ONE THING I can do to...

SMALL (reasonable, average, safe)

FIND A GREAT ANSWER

Doable: Within reach of your knowledge, skills, and experience.

Stretch: Still within your reach – the farthest end of your current abilities. Research & study others.

Possibility: Beyond what is already known and being done. Research & study others, then innovate.

Q&A SHEET

GREAT QUESTIONS LEAD TO GREAT ANSWERS.
THINK BIG AND SPECIFIC; RESEARCH AND ROLE MODEL.

ASK A GREAT QUESTION

BIG (extreme, ambitious, bold)

Big & Broad	**Big & Specific**
What's the ONE THING I can do to...	*What's the ONE THING I can do to...*
Small & Broad	**Small & Specific**
What's the ONE THING I can do to...	*What's the ONE THING I can do to...*

BROAD (general, unclear)

SPECIFIC (what, how much, until when)

SMALL (reasonable, average, safe)

FIND A GREAT ANSWER

Doable: Within reach of your knowledge, skills, and experience.

Stretch: Still within your reach — the farthest end of your current abilities. Research & study others.

Possibility: Beyond what is already known and being done. Research & study others, then innovate.

DAYDREAMERS PRINT

Q&A SHEET

GREAT QUESTIONS LEAD TO GREAT ANSWERS.
THINK BIG AND SPECIFIC; RESEARCH AND ROLE MODEL.

ASK A GREAT QUESTION

BIG (extreme, ambitious, bold)

BROAD (general, unclear)

Big & Broad	Big & Specific
What's the ONE THING I can do to...	*What's the ONE THING I can do to...*

SPECIFIC (what, how much, until when)

Small & Broad	Small & Specific
What's the ONE THING I can do to...	*What's the ONE THING I can do to...*

SMALL (reasonable, average, safe)

FIND A GREAT ANSWER

Doable: Within reach of your knowledge, skills, and experience.

Stretch: Still within your reach – the farthest end of your current abilities. Research & study others.

Possibility: Beyond what is already known and being done. Research & study others, then innovate.

DAYDREAMERS PRINT

Q&A SHEET

GREAT QUESTIONS LEAD TO GREAT ANSWERS.
THINK BIG AND SPECIFIC; RESEARCH AND ROLE MODEL.

ASK A GREAT QUESTION

BIG (extreme, ambitious, bold)

Big & Broad	**Big & Specific**
What's the ONE THING I can do to...	*What's the ONE THING I can do to...*
Small & Broad	**Small & Specific**
What's the ONE THING I can do to...	*What's the ONE THING I can do to...*

BROAD (general, unclear)

SPECIFIC (what, how much, until when)

SMALL (reasonable, average, safe)

FIND A GREAT ANSWER

Doable: Within reach of your knowledge, skills, and experience.

Stretch: Still within your reach – the farthest end of your current abilities. Research & study others.

Possibility: Beyond what is already known and being done. Research & study others, then innovate.

DAYDREAMERS PRINT

Q&A SHEET

GREAT QUESTIONS LEAD TO GREAT ANSWERS.
THINK BIG AND SPECIFIC; RESEARCH AND ROLE MODEL.

ASK A GREAT QUESTION

BIG (extreme, ambitious, bold)

Big & Broad	**Big & Specific**
What's the ONE THING I can do to...	*What's the ONE THING I can do to...*
Small & Broad	**Small & Specific**
What's the ONE THING I can do to...	*What's the ONE THING I can do to...*

BROAD (general, unclear)

SPECIFIC (what, how much, until when)

SMALL (reasonable, average, safe)

FIND A GREAT ANSWER

Doable: Within reach of your knowledge, skills, and experience.

Stretch: Still within your reach – the farthest end of your current abilities. Research & study others.

Possibility: Beyond what is already known and being done. Research & study others, then innovate.

SUCCESS HABITS
SHEET

HABIT	TIME BLOCK	66 DAYS
	?	

CHOOSE THE RIGHT HABIT AND BRING JUST ENOUGH DISCIPLINE TO ESTABLISH IT.

SUCCESS HABITS SHEET

CHOOSE THE RIGHT HABIT
AND BRING JUST ENOUGH DISCIPLINE TO ESTABLISH IT.

☑ **HABIT:** _____ **TIME BLOCK:** From: _____ To: _____

DAY 1		DAY 12		DAY 23		DAY 34		DAY 45		DAY 56	
DAY 2		DAY 13		DAY 24		DAY 35		DAY 46		DAY 57	
DAY 3		DAY 14		DAY 25		DAY 36		DAY 47		DAY 58	
DAY 4		DAY 15		DAY 26		DAY 37		DAY 48		DAY 59	
DAY 5		DAY 16		DAY 27		DAY 38		DAY 49		DAY 60	
DAY 6		DAY 17		DAY 28		DAY 39		DAY 50		DAY 61	
DAY 7		DAY 18		DAY 29		DAY 40		DAY 51		DAY 62	
DAY 8		DAY 19		DAY 30		DAY 41		DAY 52		DAY 63	
DAY 9		DAY 20		DAY 31		DAY 42		DAY 53		DAY 64	
DAY 10		DAY 21		DAY 32		DAY 43		DAY 54		DAY 65	
DAY 11		DAY 22		DAY 33		DAY 44		DAY 55		DAY 66	

☑ **HABIT:** _____ **TIME BLOCK:** From: _____ To: _____

DAY 1		DAY 12		DAY 23		DAY 34		DAY 45		DAY 56	
DAY 2		DAY 13		DAY 24		DAY 35		DAY 46		DAY 57	
DAY 3		DAY 14		DAY 25		DAY 36		DAY 47		DAY 58	
DAY 4		DAY 15		DAY 26		DAY 37		DAY 48		DAY 59	
DAY 5		DAY 16		DAY 27		DAY 38		DAY 49		DAY 60	
DAY 6		DAY 17		DAY 28		DAY 39		DAY 50		DAY 61	
DAY 7		DAY 18		DAY 29		DAY 40		DAY 51		DAY 62	
DAY 8		DAY 19		DAY 30		DAY 41		DAY 52		DAY 63	
DAY 9		DAY 20		DAY 31		DAY 42		DAY 53		DAY 64	
DAY 10		DAY 21		DAY 32		DAY 43		DAY 54		DAY 65	
DAY 11		DAY 22		DAY 33		DAY 44		DAY 55		DAY 66	

☑ **HABIT:** _____ **TIME BLOCK:** From: _____ To: _____

DAY 1		DAY 12		DAY 23		DAY 34		DAY 45		DAY 56	
DAY 2		DAY 13		DAY 24		DAY 35		DAY 46		DAY 57	
DAY 3		DAY 14		DAY 25		DAY 36		DAY 47		DAY 58	
DAY 4		DAY 15		DAY 26		DAY 37		DAY 48		DAY 59	
DAY 5		DAY 16		DAY 27		DAY 38		DAY 49		DAY 60	
DAY 6		DAY 17		DAY 28		DAY 39		DAY 50		DAY 61	
DAY 7		DAY 18		DAY 29		DAY 40		DAY 51		DAY 62	
DAY 8		DAY 19		DAY 30		DAY 41		DAY 52		DAY 63	
DAY 9		DAY 20		DAY 31		DAY 42		DAY 53		DAY 64	
DAY 10		DAY 21		DAY 32		DAY 43		DAY 54		DAY 65	
DAY 11		DAY 22		DAY 33		DAY 44		DAY 55		DAY 66	

SUCCESS HABITS SHEET

CHOOSE THE RIGHT HABIT
AND BRING JUST ENOUGH DISCIPLINE TO ESTABLISH IT.

HABIT: _____ TIME BLOCK: From: _____ To: _____

DAY 1		DAY 12		DAY 23		DAY 34		DAY 45		DAY 56	
DAY 2		DAY 13		DAY 24		DAY 35		DAY 46		DAY 57	
DAY 3		DAY 14		DAY 25		DAY 36		DAY 47		DAY 58	
DAY 4		DAY 15		DAY 26		DAY 37		DAY 48		DAY 59	
DAY 5		DAY 16		DAY 27		DAY 38		DAY 49		DAY 60	
DAY 6		DAY 17		DAY 28		DAY 39		DAY 50		DAY 61	
DAY 7		DAY 18		DAY 29		DAY 40		DAY 51		DAY 62	
DAY 8		DAY 19		DAY 30		DAY 41		DAY 52		DAY 63	
DAY 9		DAY 20		DAY 31		DAY 42		DAY 53		DAY 64	
DAY 10		DAY 21		DAY 32		DAY 43		DAY 54		DAY 65	
DAY 11		DAY 22		DAY 33		DAY 44		DAY 55		DAY 66	

HABIT: _____ TIME BLOCK: From: _____ To: _____

DAY 1		DAY 12		DAY 23		DAY 34		DAY 45		DAY 56	
DAY 2		DAY 13		DAY 24		DAY 35		DAY 46		DAY 57	
DAY 3		DAY 14		DAY 25		DAY 36		DAY 47		DAY 58	
DAY 4		DAY 15		DAY 26		DAY 37		DAY 48		DAY 59	
DAY 5		DAY 16		DAY 27		DAY 38		DAY 49		DAY 60	
DAY 6		DAY 17		DAY 28		DAY 39		DAY 50		DAY 61	
DAY 7		DAY 18		DAY 29		DAY 40		DAY 51		DAY 62	
DAY 8		DAY 19		DAY 30		DAY 41		DAY 52		DAY 63	
DAY 9		DAY 20		DAY 31		DAY 42		DAY 53		DAY 64	
DAY 10		DAY 21		DAY 32		DAY 43		DAY 54		DAY 65	
DAY 11		DAY 22		DAY 33		DAY 44		DAY 55		DAY 66	

HABIT: _____ TIME BLOCK: From: _____ To: _____

DAY 1		DAY 12		DAY 23		DAY 34		DAY 45		DAY 56	
DAY 2		DAY 13		DAY 24		DAY 35		DAY 46		DAY 57	
DAY 3		DAY 14		DAY 25		DAY 36		DAY 47		DAY 58	
DAY 4		DAY 15		DAY 26		DAY 37		DAY 48		DAY 59	
DAY 5		DAY 16		DAY 27		DAY 38		DAY 49		DAY 60	
DAY 6		DAY 17		DAY 28		DAY 39		DAY 50		DAY 61	
DAY 7		DAY 18		DAY 29		DAY 40		DAY 51		DAY 62	
DAY 8		DAY 19		DAY 30		DAY 41		DAY 52		DAY 63	
DAY 9		DAY 20		DAY 31		DAY 42		DAY 53		DAY 64	
DAY 10		DAY 21		DAY 32		DAY 43		DAY 54		DAY 65	
DAY 11		DAY 22		DAY 33		DAY 44		DAY 55		DAY 66	

SUCCESS HABITS SHEET

CHOOSE THE RIGHT HABIT
AND BRING JUST ENOUGH DISCIPLINE TO ESTABLISH IT.

HABIT: _____   **TIME BLOCK:** From: _____ To: _____

DAY 1		DAY 12		DAY 23		DAY 34		DAY 45		DAY 56	
DAY 2		DAY 13		DAY 24		DAY 35		DAY 46		DAY 57	
DAY 3		DAY 14		DAY 25		DAY 36		DAY 47		DAY 58	
DAY 4		DAY 15		DAY 26		DAY 37		DAY 48		DAY 59	
DAY 5		DAY 16		DAY 27		DAY 38		DAY 49		DAY 60	
DAY 6		DAY 17		DAY 28		DAY 39		DAY 50		DAY 61	
DAY 7		DAY 18		DAY 29		DAY 40		DAY 51		DAY 62	
DAY 8		DAY 19		DAY 30		DAY 41		DAY 52		DAY 63	
DAY 9		DAY 20		DAY 31		DAY 42		DAY 53		DAY 64	
DAY 10		DAY 21		DAY 32		DAY 43		DAY 54		DAY 65	
DAY 11		DAY 22		DAY 33		DAY 44		DAY 55		DAY 66	

HABIT: _____   **TIME BLOCK:** From: _____ To: _____

DAY 1		DAY 12		DAY 23		DAY 34		DAY 45		DAY 56	
DAY 2		DAY 13		DAY 24		DAY 35		DAY 46		DAY 57	
DAY 3		DAY 14		DAY 25		DAY 36		DAY 47		DAY 58	
DAY 4		DAY 15		DAY 26		DAY 37		DAY 48		DAY 59	
DAY 5		DAY 16		DAY 27		DAY 38		DAY 49		DAY 60	
DAY 6		DAY 17		DAY 28		DAY 39		DAY 50		DAY 61	
DAY 7		DAY 18		DAY 29		DAY 40		DAY 51		DAY 62	
DAY 8		DAY 19		DAY 30		DAY 41		DAY 52		DAY 63	
DAY 9		DAY 20		DAY 31		DAY 42		DAY 53		DAY 64	
DAY 10		DAY 21		DAY 32		DAY 43		DAY 54		DAY 65	
DAY 11		DAY 22		DAY 33		DAY 44		DAY 55		DAY 66	

HABIT: _____   **TIME BLOCK:** From: _____ To: _____

DAY 1		DAY 12		DAY 23		DAY 34		DAY 45		DAY 56	
DAY 2		DAY 13		DAY 24		DAY 35		DAY 46		DAY 57	
DAY 3		DAY 14		DAY 25		DAY 36		DAY 47		DAY 58	
DAY 4		DAY 15		DAY 26		DAY 37		DAY 48		DAY 59	
DAY 5		DAY 16		DAY 27		DAY 38		DAY 49		DAY 60	
DAY 6		DAY 17		DAY 28		DAY 39		DAY 50		DAY 61	
DAY 7		DAY 18		DAY 29		DAY 40		DAY 51		DAY 62	
DAY 8		DAY 19		DAY 30		DAY 41		DAY 52		DAY 63	
DAY 9		DAY 20		DAY 31		DAY 42		DAY 53		DAY 64	
DAY 10		DAY 21		DAY 32		DAY 43		DAY 54		DAY 65	
DAY 11		DAY 22		DAY 33		DAY 44		DAY 55		DAY 66	

Made in the USA
Las Vegas, NV
02 November 2021